voces 8

A CAPPELLA SONGBOOK 2

Eight songs for four-part vocal groups | Acht Songs für vierstimmiges Vokalensemble

ALLE RECHTE VORBEHALTEN · ALL RIGHTS RESERVED

EDITION PETERS

LEIPZIG · LONDON · NEW YORK

This edition © 2018 by Peters Edition Ltd, London

All rights reserved. No part of this publication may be reproduced,
stored in a retrieval system or transmitted in any form or by any means,
electronic, mechanical, photocopying, recording or otherwise, without the
prior written permission of the publisher.

Das Werk und seine Teile sind urheberrechtlich geschützt.
Jede Nutzung in anderen als den gesetzlich zugelassenen Fällen
bedarf der vorherigen schriftlichen Einwilligung des Verlages.
Hinweis zu § 52a UrhG: Weder das Werk noch seine Teile dürfen ohne
eine solche Einwilligung eingescannt und in ein Netzwerk gestellt werden.

Peters Edition Ltd
2–6 Baches Street
London
N1 6DN
Tel: 020 7553 4000
email: www.sales@editionpeters.com
web: www.editionpeters.com

Cover photo: Andy Staples

Contents | Inhalt

Song Introductions | Einführungen zu den Songs — 2

Atlantic Avenue — 4
Written by Alan Gorrie, Roger Ball,
Hamish Stuart, Owen McIntyre, Stephen Ferrone
arr. Emily Dickens and Dingle Yandell

Danny Boy — 19
Traditional Irish arr. Joshua Pacey

Edo Lullaby — 28
Traditional Japanese arr. Paul Smith

My love is like a red, red rose — 33
Pietro Urbani arr. Jim Clements

Pie Jesu — 39
Gabriel Fauré arr. Barnaby Smith

Price Tag — 45
Words and Music by Claude Kelly, Bobby Ray Simmons Jr,
Lukasz Gottwald and Jessica Cornish
arr. Andrea Halsey

Strong — 60
Words and Music by Hannah Reid,
Dominic Major and Daniel Rothman
arr. Emily Dickens and Dingle Yandell

Underneath the Stars — 72
Kate Rusby arr. Jim Clements

Song Introductions | Einführungen zu den Songs

Atlantic Avenue

We first used this funk tune by the Average White Band for one of the summer school weeks we run each year at Milton Abbey in the UK. Emily Dickens and Dingle Yandell wrote the arrangement for their chamber music group and it became an instant hit with participants and us alike. This is a fun-filled song bursting with South American rhythm and more than a dash of summer sunshine!

Danny Boy

Originally written to a different tune by Frederick Weatherly in 1910, Danny Boy was adapted to fit to the tune 'Londonderry Air' in 1913 and the first recording was produced in 1915. The song, possibly written as a message from a parent to a son going off to war or uprising, or possibly leaving as part of the Irish diaspora, has been covered by many singers – from Mario Lanza to Jonny Cash, Harry Belafonte to Tom Jones.

Edo Lullaby

This traditional cradle song from Japan originated in Edo, the old name for modern day Tokyo, and the seat of power in the 17th and 18th centuries. The beautiful melody was first introduced to us by Roxanna Panufnik, and we created this arrangement for a trip to Tokyo in 2016. Here is a translation of the text:

Hushabye, hushabye! / My good baby, sleep! / Where did my boy's baby-sitter go? / Beyond that mountain, back to her home. / As a souvenir from her home, what did you get? / A toy drum and a shō flute.

My love is like a red, red rose

Created by Robert Burns in the Scots language in 1794, and based on traditional sources, Burns gave this song to singer Pietro Urbani who published it in his *Scots Songs*. In his book, Urbani claimed 'the words of *The Red Red Rose* were obligingly given to him by a celebrated Scots poet, who was so struck by them when sung by a country girl that he wrote them down and, not being pleased with the air, begged the author to set them to music in the style of a Scots tune, which he has done accordingly'.

Atlantic Avenue

Diesen Funk-Titel der Average White Band haben wir zuerst bei einem unserer einwöchigen Sommerkurse verwendet, die jedes Jahr in Milton Abbey (Südengland) stattfinden. Emily Dickens und Dingle Yandell haben dort für ihre Kammermusikgruppe dieses Arrangement geschaffen, das bei den Kursteilnehmern sofort auf ebenso große Begeisterung stieß wie bei uns selbst. Ein ausgelassenes Lied voll südamerikanischer Rhythmen und mit einer gehörigen Portion Sonnenschein!

Danny Boy

Der Text dieses Lieds wurde 1910 von Frederick Weatherly zunächst zu einer anderen Melodie verfasst, ehe 1913 eine abgewandelte Fassung auf die Volksweise „Londonderry Air" entstand. In dieser Form wurde das Stück schon 1915 erstmals aufgenommen. Möglicherweise ist es als Abschiedsbotschaft an einen Sohn gedacht, der in den Krieg zieht, an einem Aufstand teilnimmt oder auch – wie so viele Iren – das Land als Auswanderer verlässt. Zu den vielen Interpreten des Titels zählen Mario Lanza und Jonny Cash ebenso wie Harry Belafonte und Tom Jones.

Edo Lullaby

Dieses traditionelle Wiegenlied stammt aus Edo, dem heutigen Tokio, das im 17. und 18. Jahrhundert Machtzentrum Japans war. Nachdem uns Roxanna Panufnik mit dieser wunderschönen Melodie vertraut gemacht hatte, entstand 2016 anlässlich einer Konzertreise nach Tokio das vorliegende Arrangement. Ins Deutsche übersetzt lautet der Text:

Ei, ei, ei! / Mein liebes Kind, schlaf ein. / Wo ist das Kindermädchen meines Sohnes hin? / Hinter die Berge in die Heimat. / Was hast du als Erinnerung aus ihrer Heimat bekommen? / Eine Spielzeugtrommel und eine Shō-Flöte.

My love is like a red, red rose

Ein Lied in der Sprache des schottischen Tieflands, „Scots" genannt. Gedichtet wurde es 1794 von Robert Burns in Anlehnung an traditionelle Vorlagen. Burns gab das Lied dem Sänger Pietro Urbani, einem Spezialisten für Scots, der es in seiner Sammlung *Scots Songs* veröffentlichte. Urbani schreibt dazu, ihm sei „der Text zu *The Red Red Rose* von einem berühmten schottischen Dichter anvertraut worden, welcher von den Worten, als sie aus der Kehle eines Bauernmädchens hörte, so ergriffen war, dass er sie niederschrieb, und welcher, da ihm die Melodie nicht gefiel, den Autor anflehte, sie im Stile eines schottischen Liedes zu vertonen, was hiermit geschehen ist".

Pie Jesu

Fauré's first version of the Requiem featured five movements, of which the Pie Jesu was one, and was first performed in 1888 at a funeral at La Madeleine church in Paris. This arrangement features additional optional plainchant which frames the traditional version of the music. This a cappella setting works particularly well in venues with a generous acoustic.

Price Tag

This Jessie J hit song reached No. 1 in the UK Charts in 2011 and charted at No. 1 in 19 other countries. We began creating our arrangement of it for some of our education workshops, and such was its success that it got transferred into our stage programmes. It's an 'up-tempo, feel-good track inflected with a reggae bounce and a sing-along chorus'. Do have fun getting the audience involved in the call-and-response section of the song!

Strong

Written by the British trip hop trio, London Grammar, this song was originally arranged for one of the workshop groups at the VOCES8 International Summer School at Milton Abbey in 2016. It proved an instant hit with the group and participants, and we've been performing it around the world ever since.

Underneath the Stars

Underneath the Stars, in this beautiful arrangement by Jim Clements, is one of the most requested songs in the VOCES8 repertoire. We have always loved singing it, and are delighted to be able to share it now so that other choirs and vocal groups can enjoy performing it just as much as we do. Should you wish to hear our version, you can find it on our album *Eventide* on the Decca Classics label.

Pie Jesu

Die erste Fassung von Faurés Requiem bestand aus fünf Sätzen, darunter das Pic Jesu, und wurde 1888 bei einer Trauerfeier in der Kirche La Madeleine in Paris uraufgeführt. Im vorliegenden Arrangement wird das eigentliche Stück von Zusatzpassagen im gregorianischen Stil umrahmt, die auf den Kontext des Requiems verweisen. Der zauberhafte A-cappella-Satz kommt am besten an Orten mit üppiger Akustik zur Geltung.

Price Tag

Dieser Hit von Jessie J erreichte 2011 die Spitze der britischen Charts und stand auch in 19 weiteren Ländern auf Nummer 1. Unser Arrangement war anfangs für unsere Gesangsworkshops gedacht, hatte aber solchen Erfolg, dass wir es auch in unser Bühnenprogramm aufgenommen haben. Ein gut gelaunter Up-Tempo-Titel mit federndem Reggae-Feel und einem Refrain, der zum Mitsingen einlädt. Großen Spaß macht es, im Call-and-Response-Abschnitt das Publikum mit einzubeziehen.

Strong

Ein Song des britischen Trip-Hop-Trios London Grammar, den wir ursprünglich 2016 für eine der Workshop-Gruppen beim Internationalen Sommerkurs von VOCES8 in Milton Abbey arrangiert haben. Bei den Teilnehmern und bei uns selbst war er schnell so beliebt, dass wir ihn mittlerweile in aller Welt zu Gehör gebracht haben.

Underneath the Stars

In der herrlichen Bearbeitung von Jim Clements ist *Underneath the Stars* einer der häufigsten Wunschtitel im Repertoire von VOCES8. Wir haben ihn immer schon gerne gesungen und freuen uns, ihn hiermit auch anderen Chören und Gesangsensembles zugänglich zu machen, damit sie ebenso großen Spaß daran haben wie wir. Unsere Interpretation des Songs ist übrigens auf dem bei Decca Classics erschienenen Album *Eventide* zu hören.

Atlantic Avenue

Written by Alan Gorrie, Roger Ball,
Hamish Stuart, Owen McIntyre, Stephen Ferrone
arr. Emily Dickens and Dingle Yandell

© 1979, Published by Wixen Music UK Ltd, obo Wixen Music Publishing, Inc. as agent for Joe's Songs Inc (ASCAP)
All Rights Reserved. Used by Permission.

Atlantic Avenue | 5

8 | Atlantic Avenue

Edition Peters

10 | Atlantic Avenue

Edition Peters

12 | Atlantic Avenue

Atlantic Avenue | 13

18 | Atlantic Avenue

Danny Boy

Frederic Weatherly (1848–1929)

Traditional Irish ('Londonderry Air')
arr. Joshua Pacey

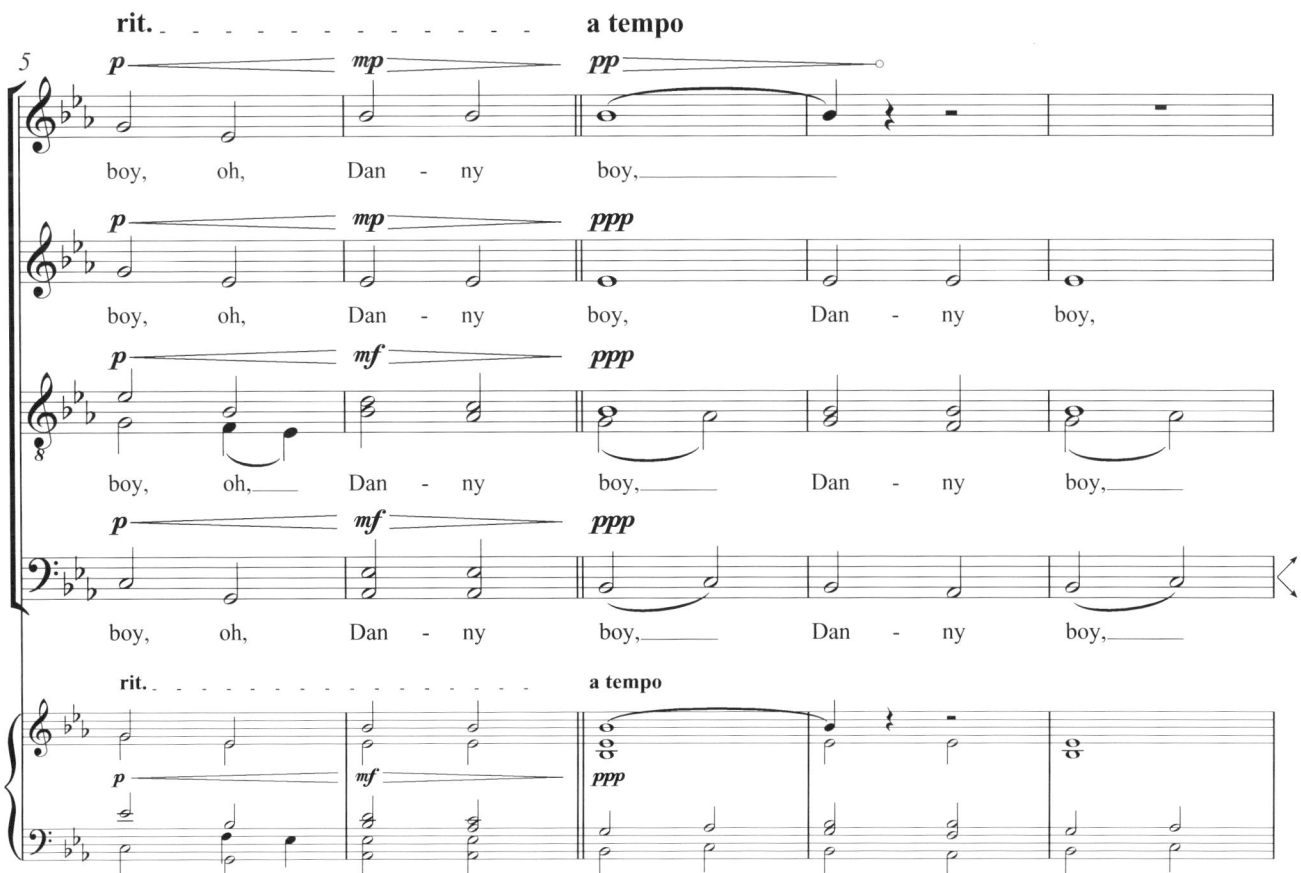

© 2017 by Peters Edition Ltd, London

20 | Danny Boy

Edition Peters

22 | Danny Boy

Edition Peters

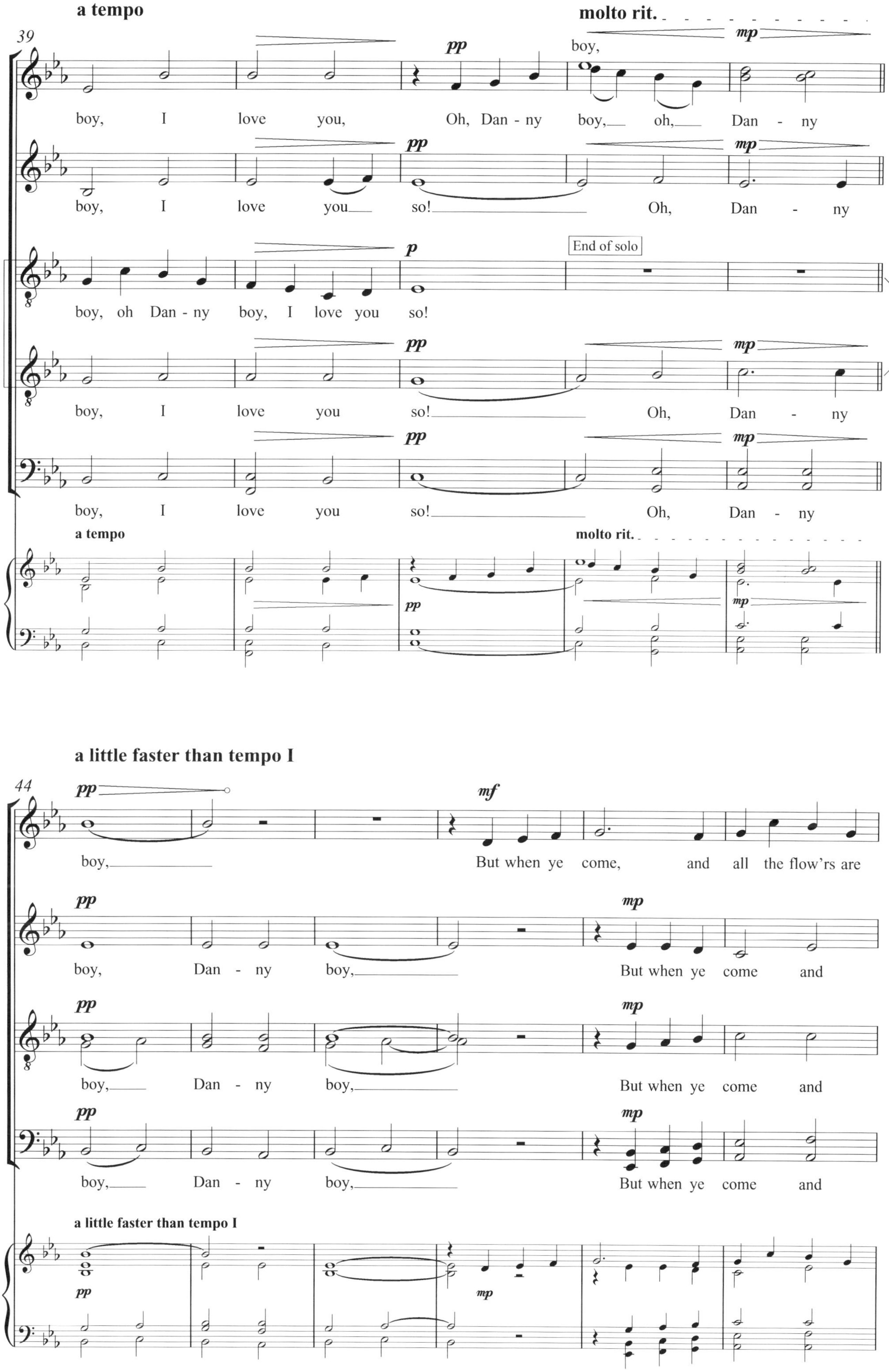
a tempo
molto rit.
39
boy,
boy, I love you, Oh, Dan - ny boy, oh, Dan - ny
boy, I love you so! Oh, Dan - ny
End of solo
boy, oh Dan - ny boy, I love you so!
boy, I love you so! Oh, Dan - ny
boy, I love you so! Oh, Dan - ny
a tempo
molto rit.
a little faster than tempo I
44
boy, But when ye come, and all the flow'rs are
boy, Dan - ny boy, But when ye come and
boy, Dan - ny boy, But when ye come and
boy, Dan - ny boy, But when ye come and
a little faster than tempo I

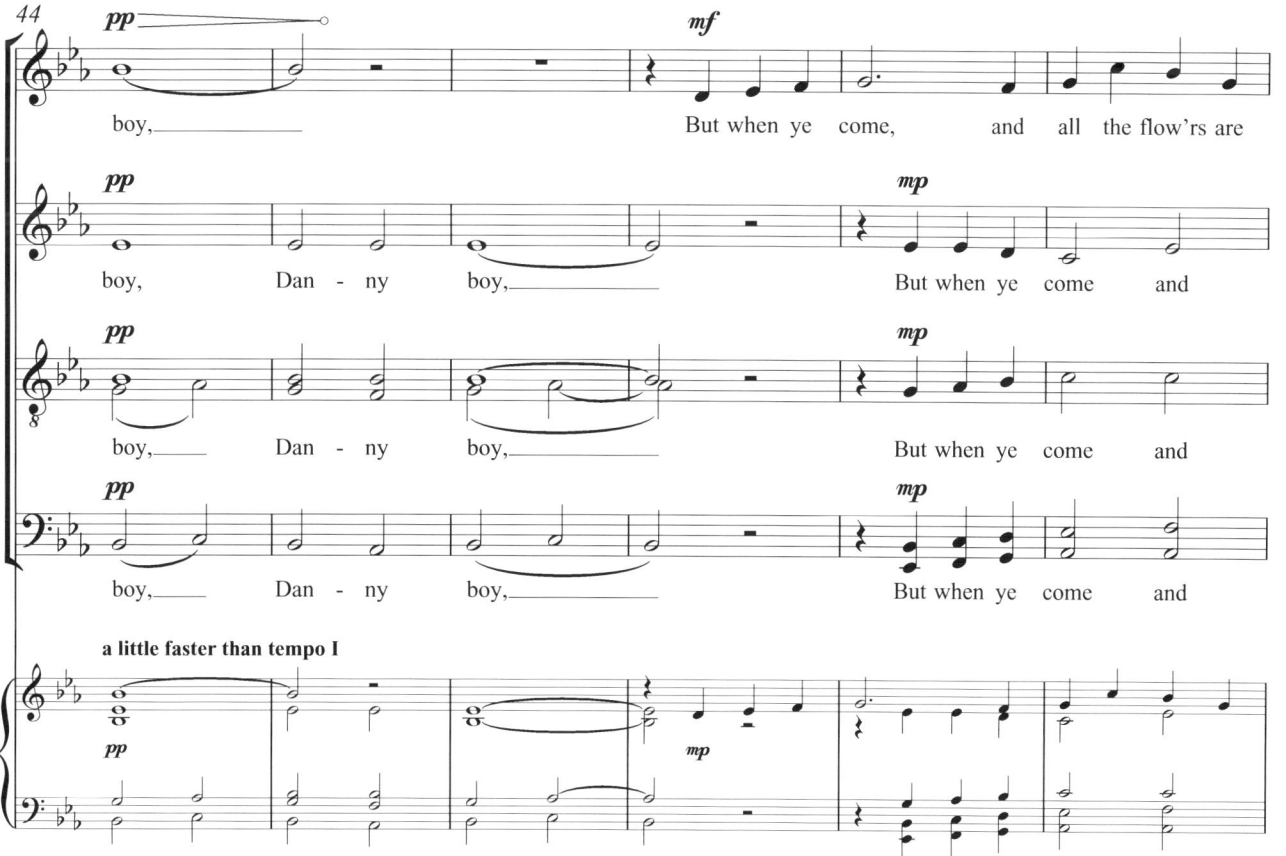

24 | Danny Boy

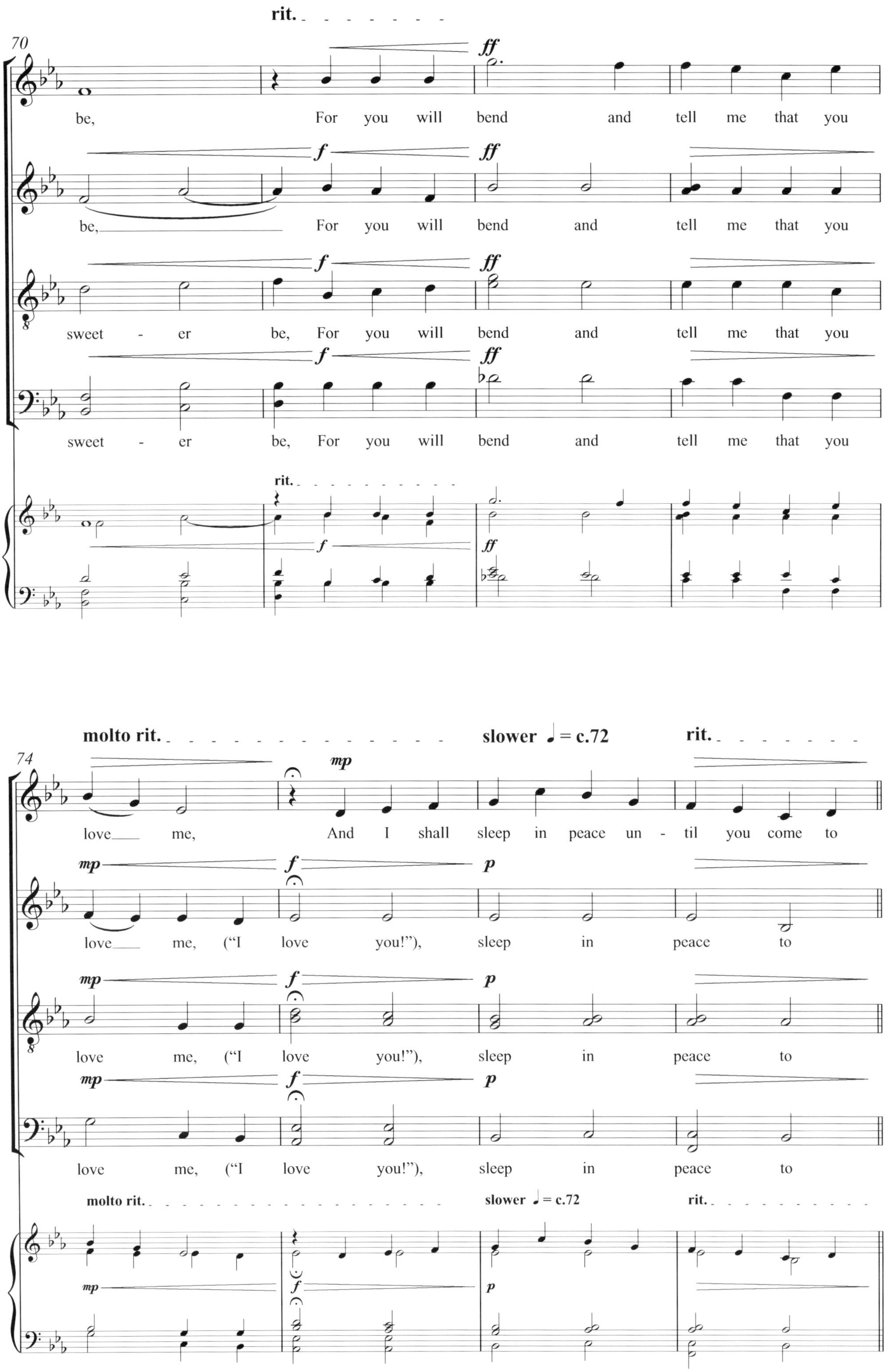
rit.
70
be, For you will bend and tell me that you
be, For you will bend and tell me that you
sweet - er be, For you will bend and tell me that you
sweet - er be, For you will bend and tell me that you
ff
f
rit.
molto rit.
slower ♩ = c.72
rit.
74
mp
love me, And I shall sleep in peace un - til you come to
love me, ("I love you!"), sleep in peace to
love me, ("I love you!"), sleep in peace to
love me, ("I love you!"), sleep in peace to
mp
f
p
molto rit.
slower ♩ = c.72
rit.

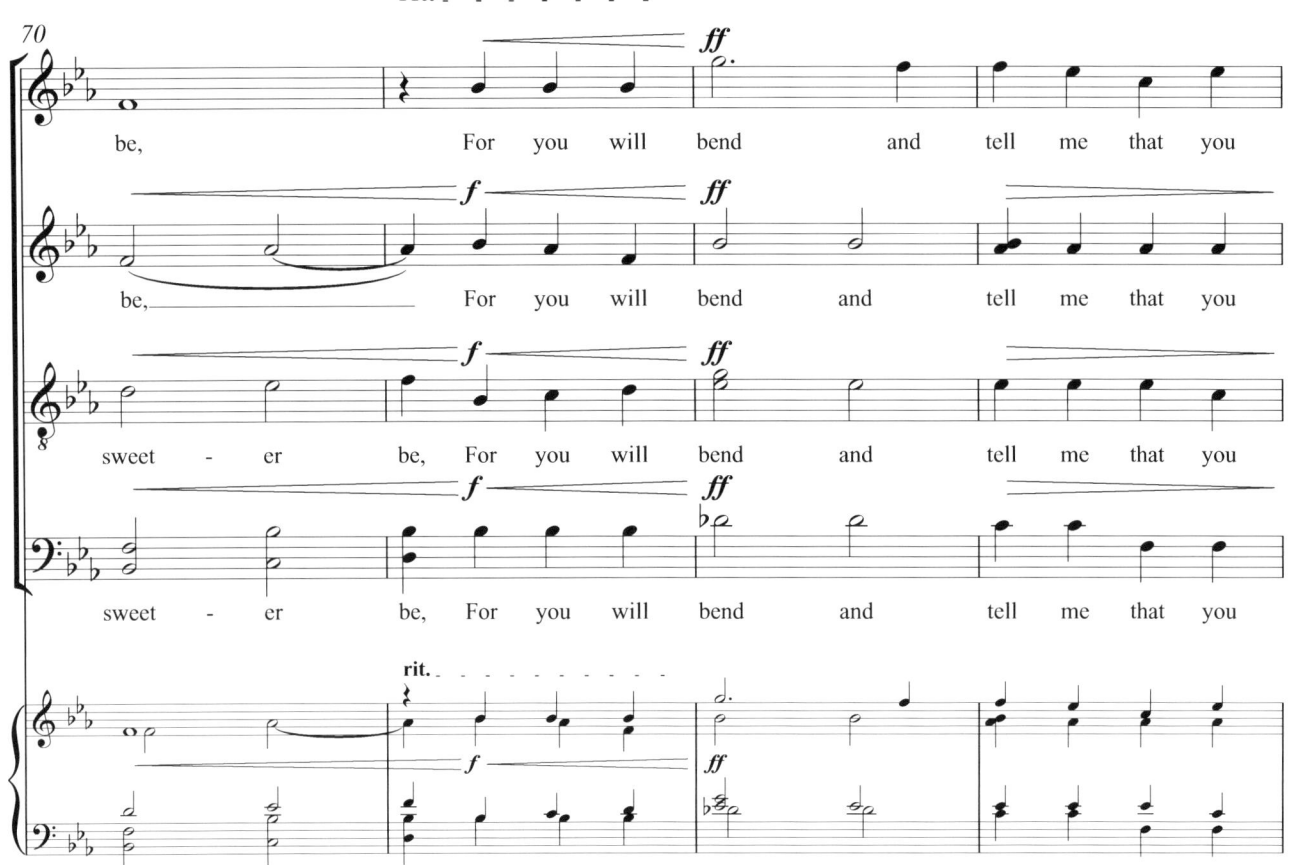

tempo I
molto rit.
78
pp
mp
p
me! Oh, Dan - ny boy, oh,
me! Oh, Dan - ny, oh, Dan - ny boy, oh,
me! Oh, Dan - ny boy, Dan - ny boy, oh,
me! Oh, Dan - ny boy, oh,
tempo I
molto rit.

83
mp
pp
mf
Dan - ny boy!
Dan - ny boy, boy!
Dan - ny boy, Dan - ny, boy!
Dan - ny boy, Dan - ny, boy!

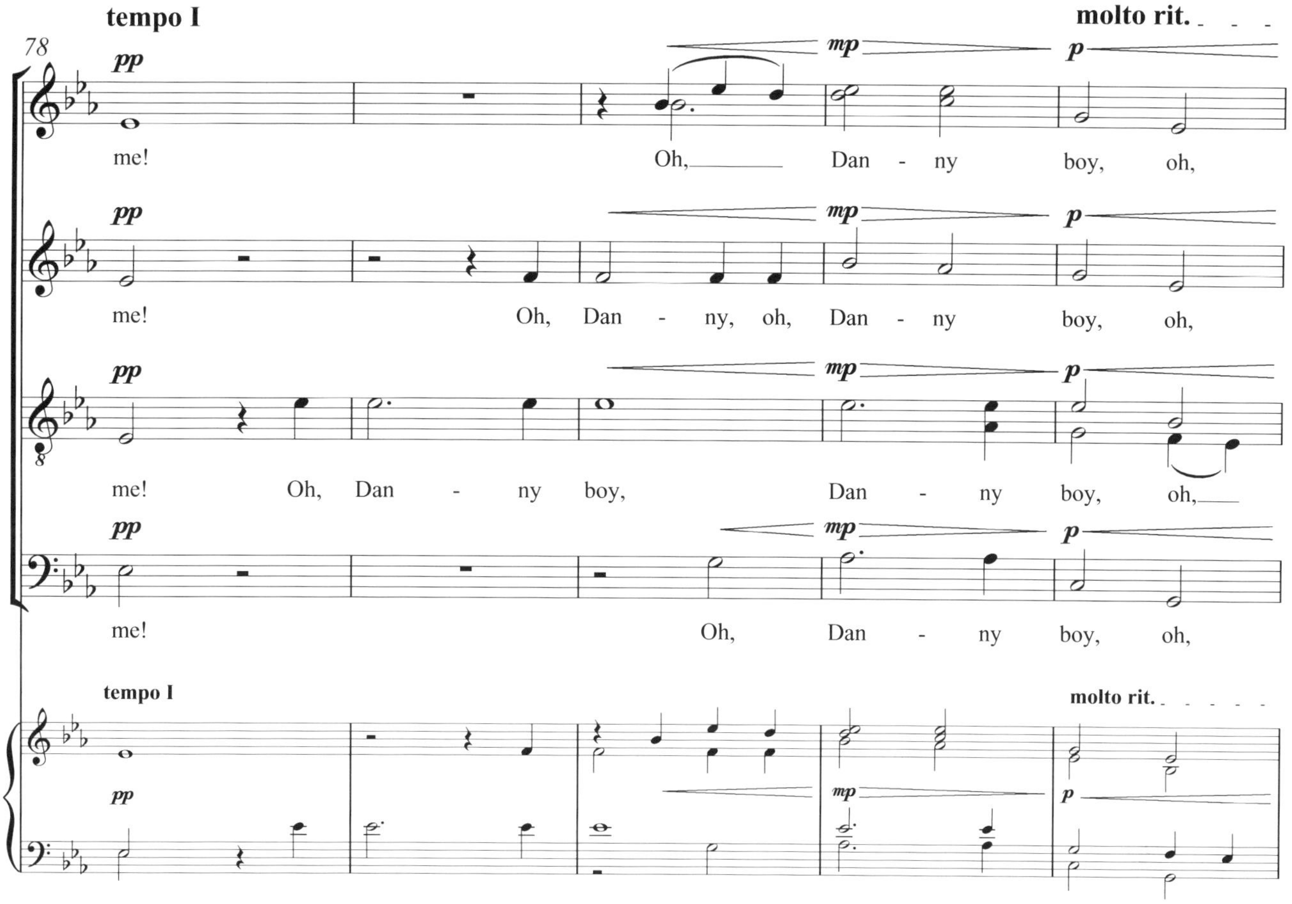

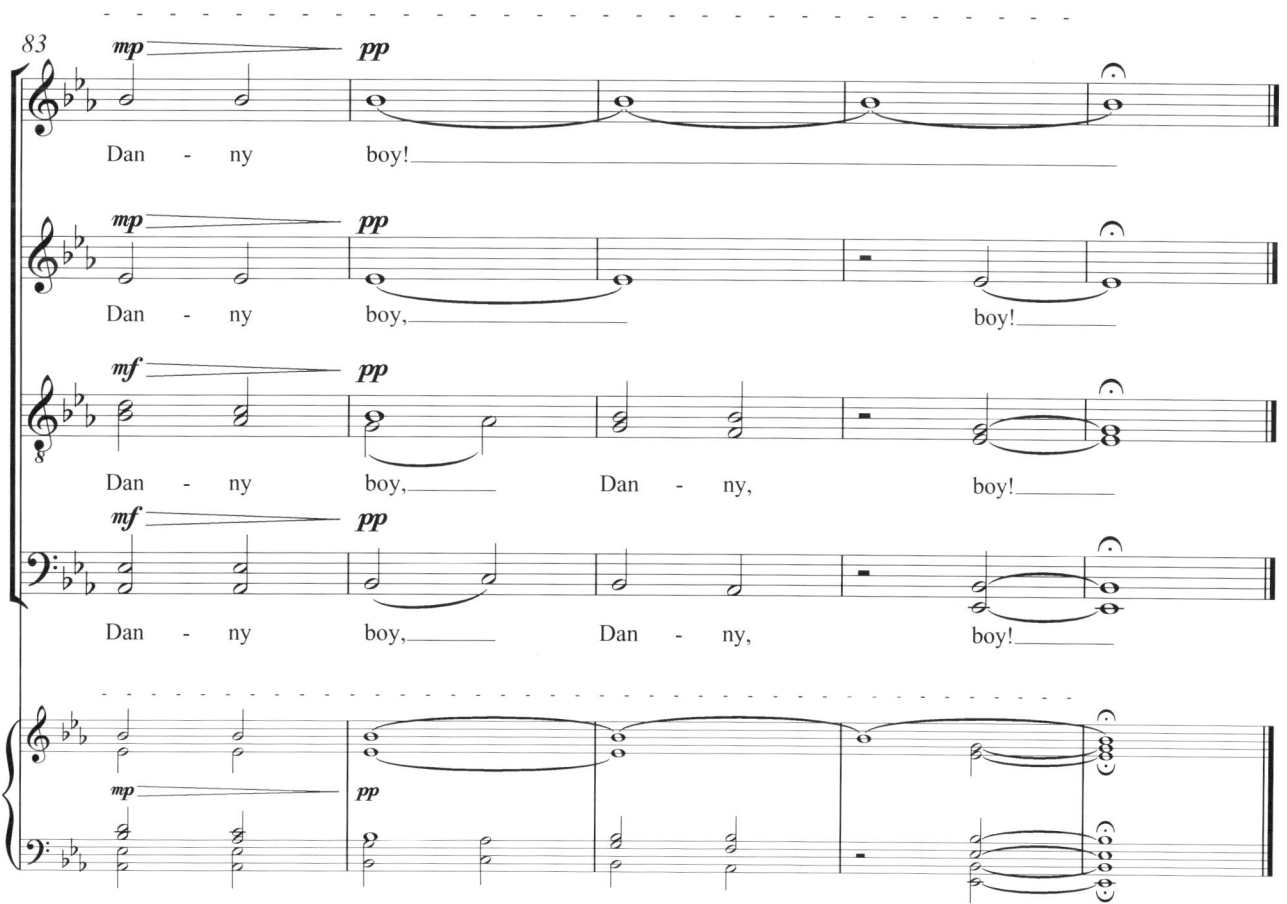

Edo Lullaby

Edo Lullaby | 29

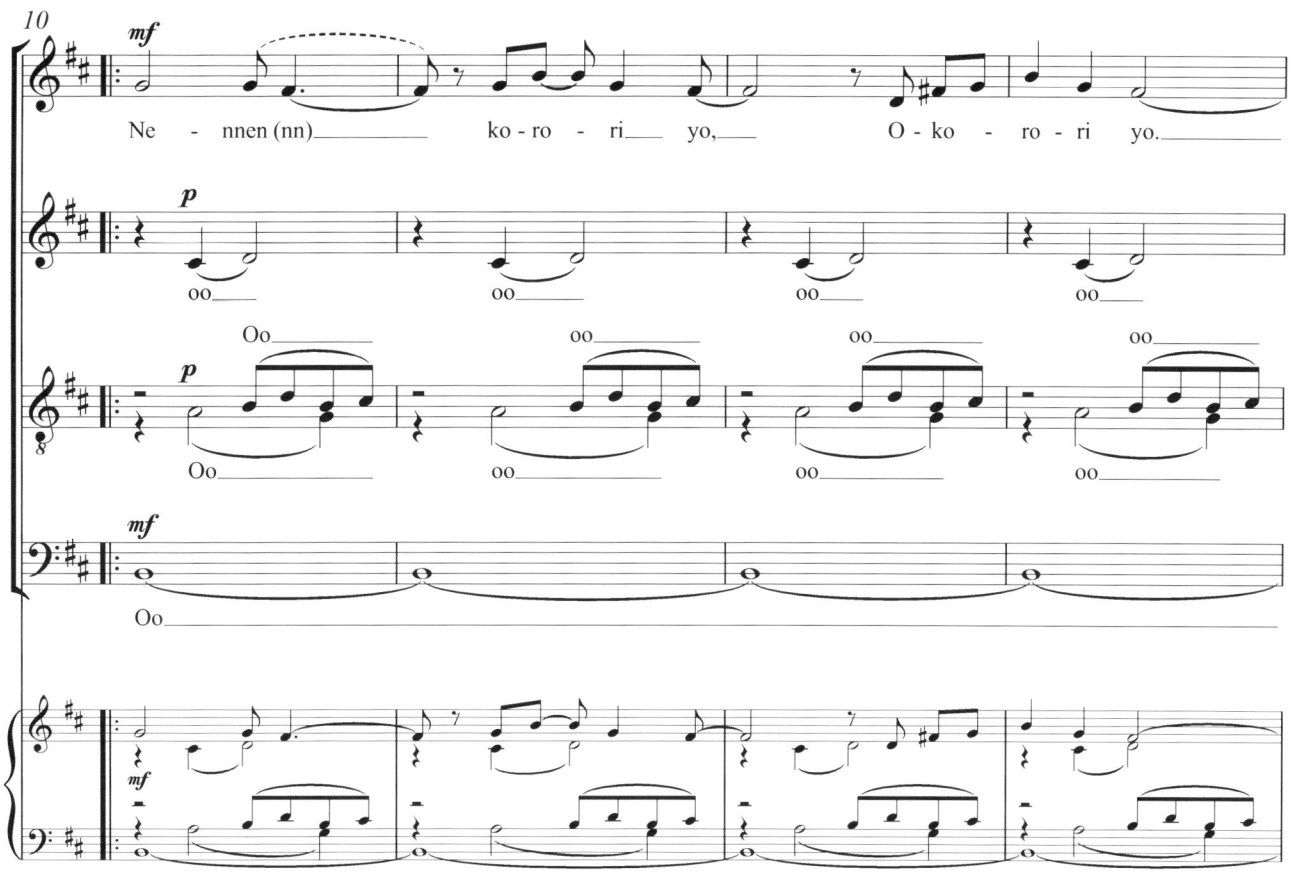
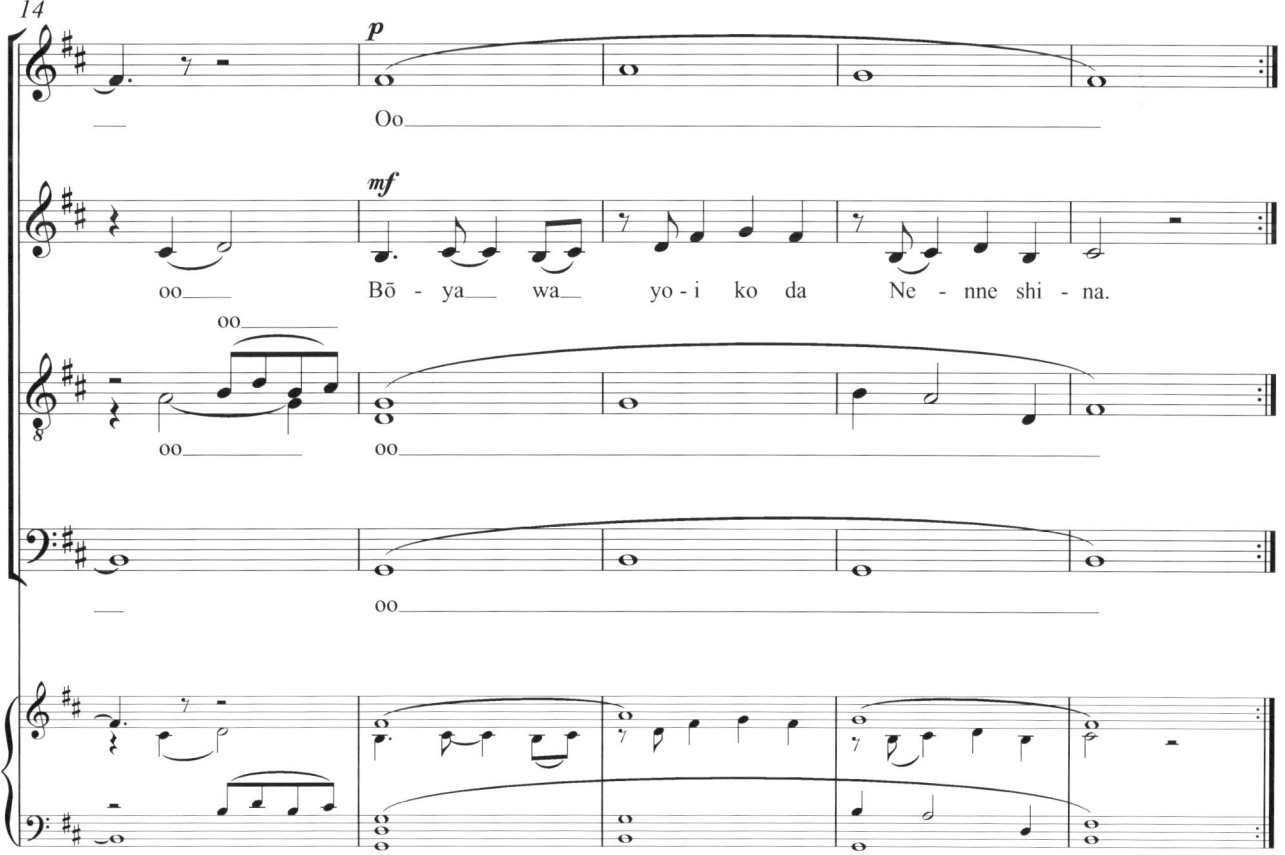

Edition Peters

30 | Edo Lullaby

32 | Edo Lullaby

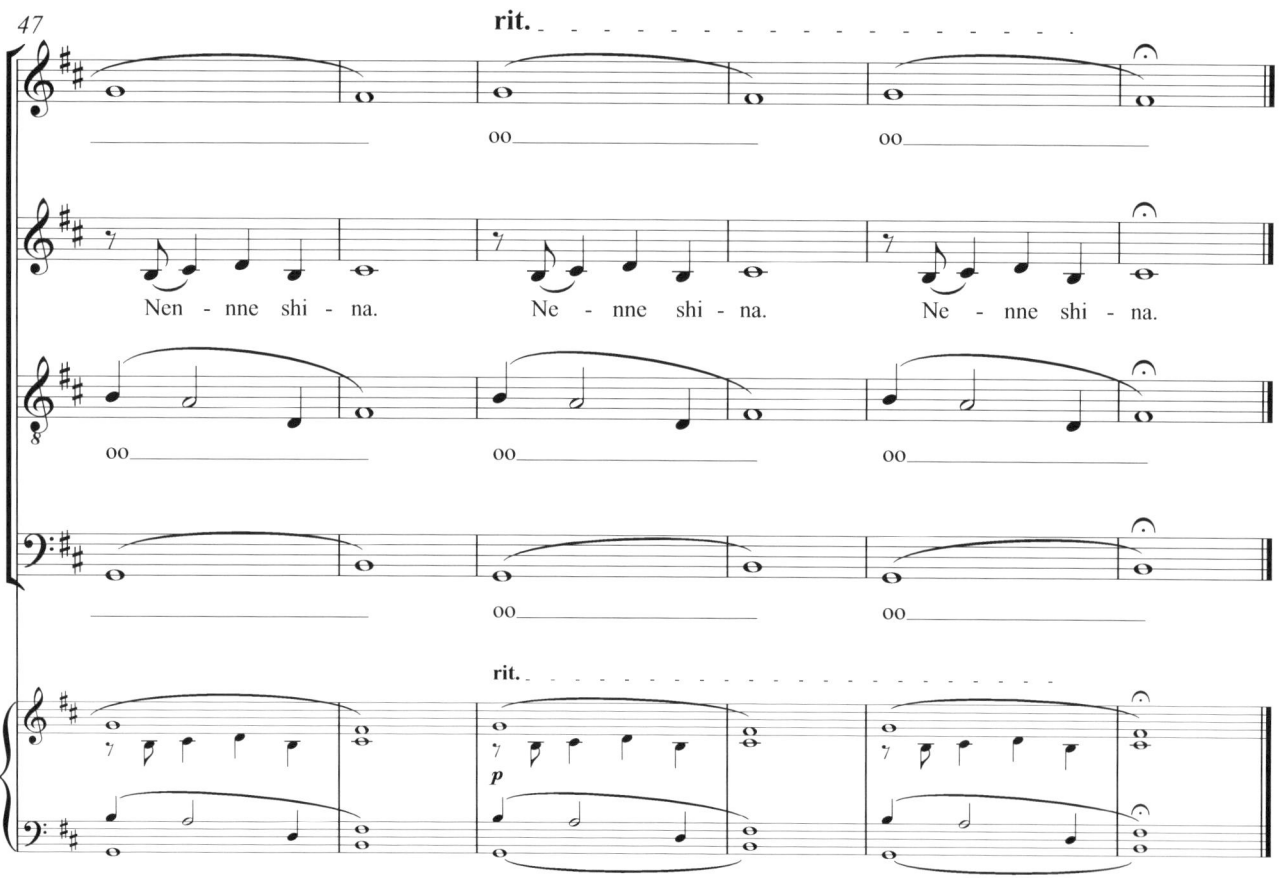

Edition Peters

My love is like a red, red rose

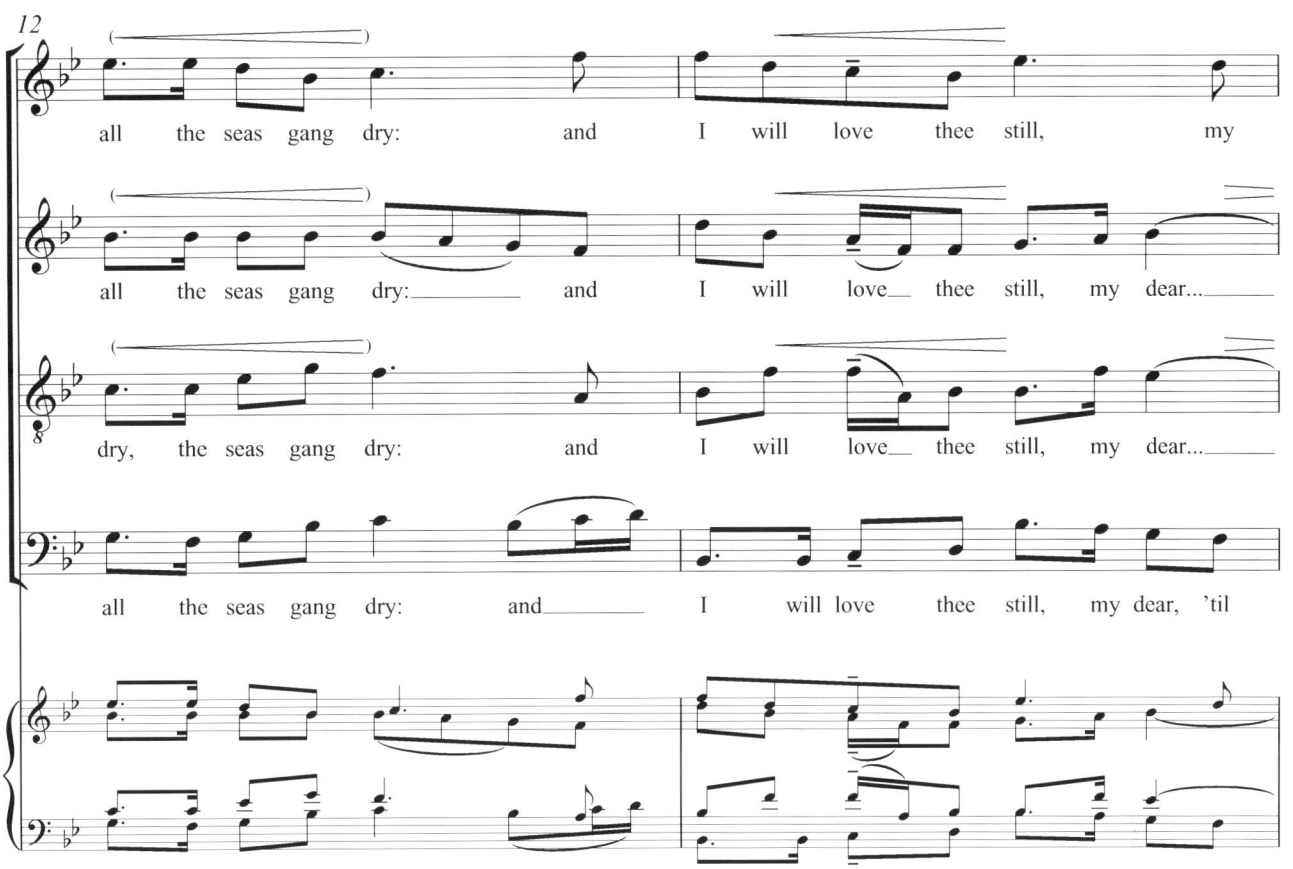

Edition Peters

36 | My love is like a red, red rose

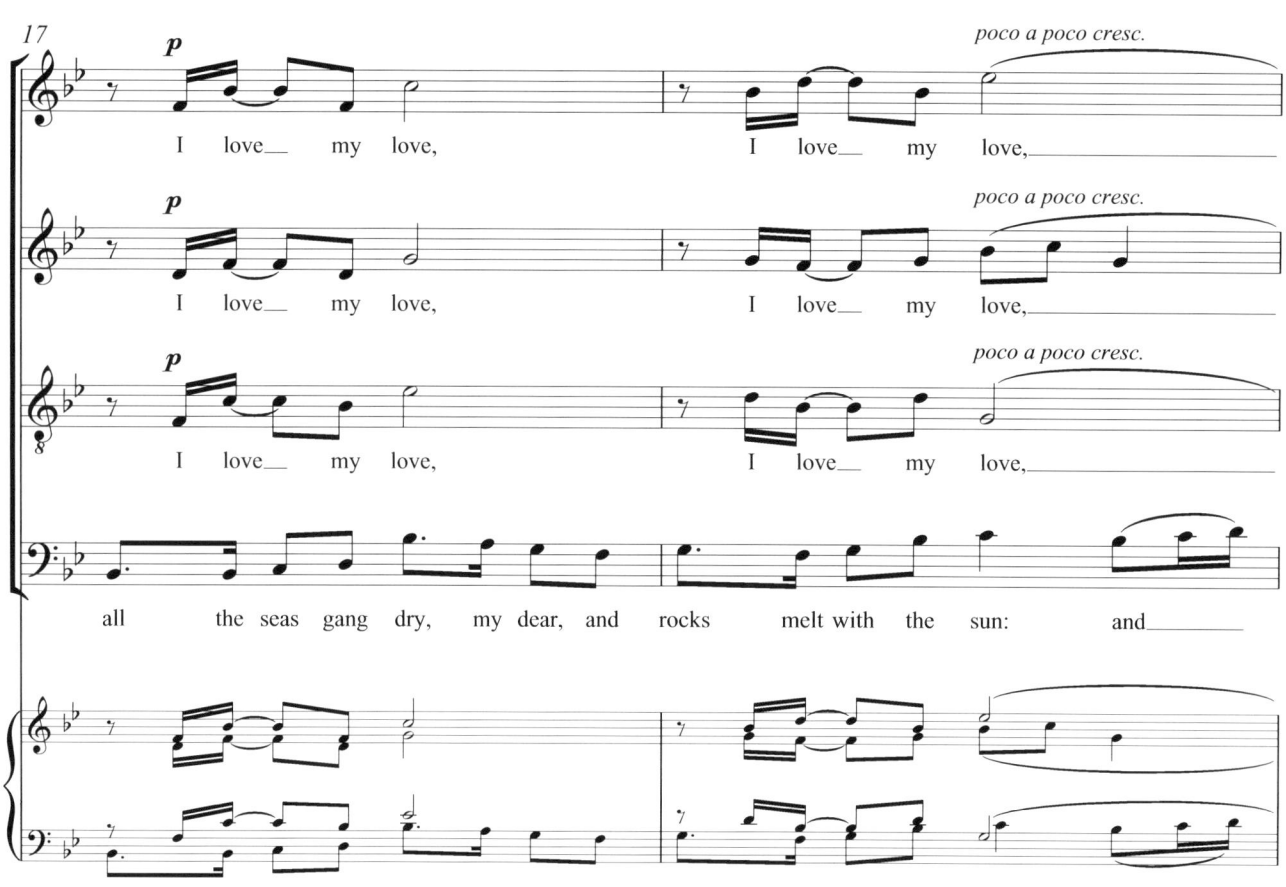

Edition Peters

My love is like a red, red rose | 37

Edition Peters

38 | My love is like a red, red rose

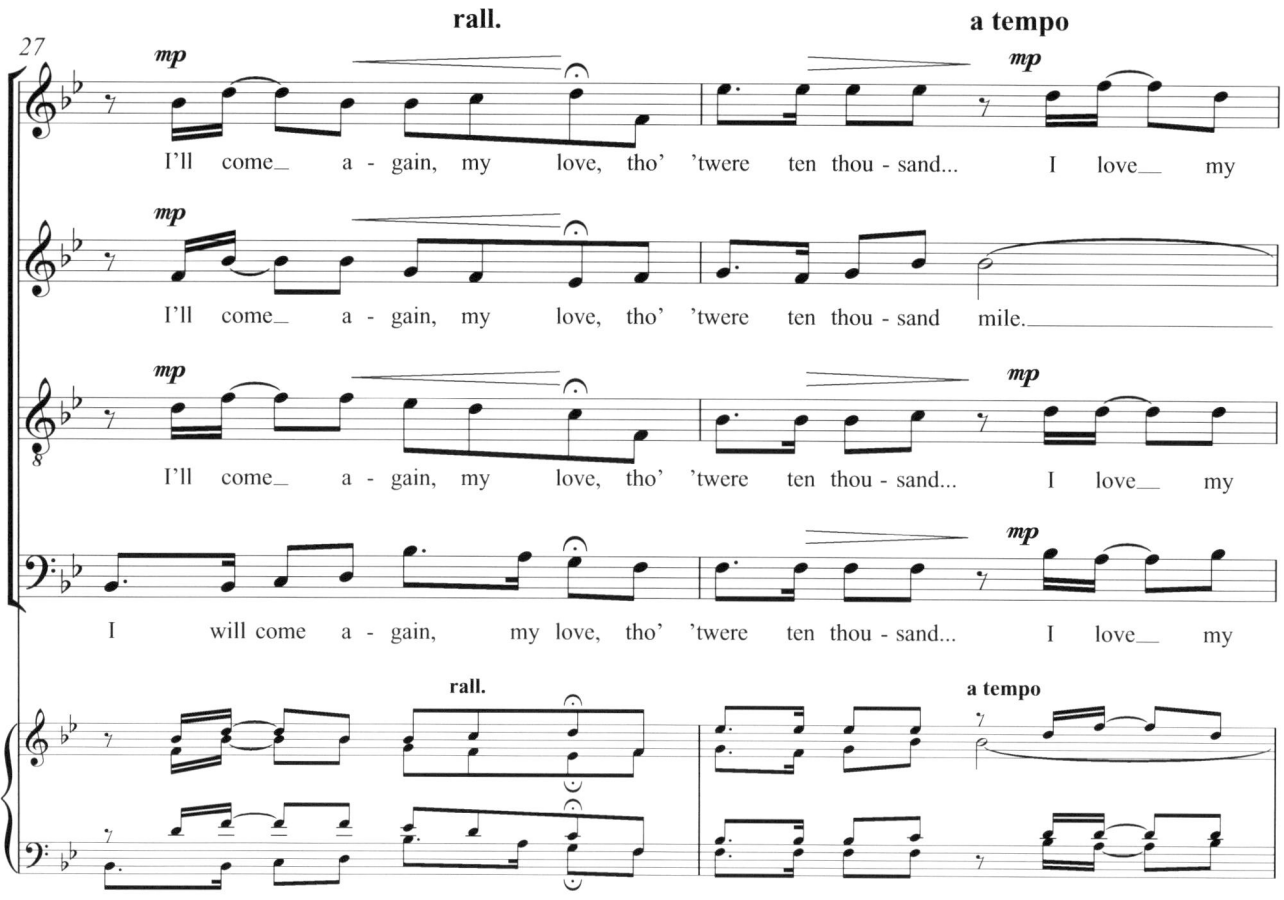

Pie Jesu

Gabriel Fauré
arr. Barnaby Smith

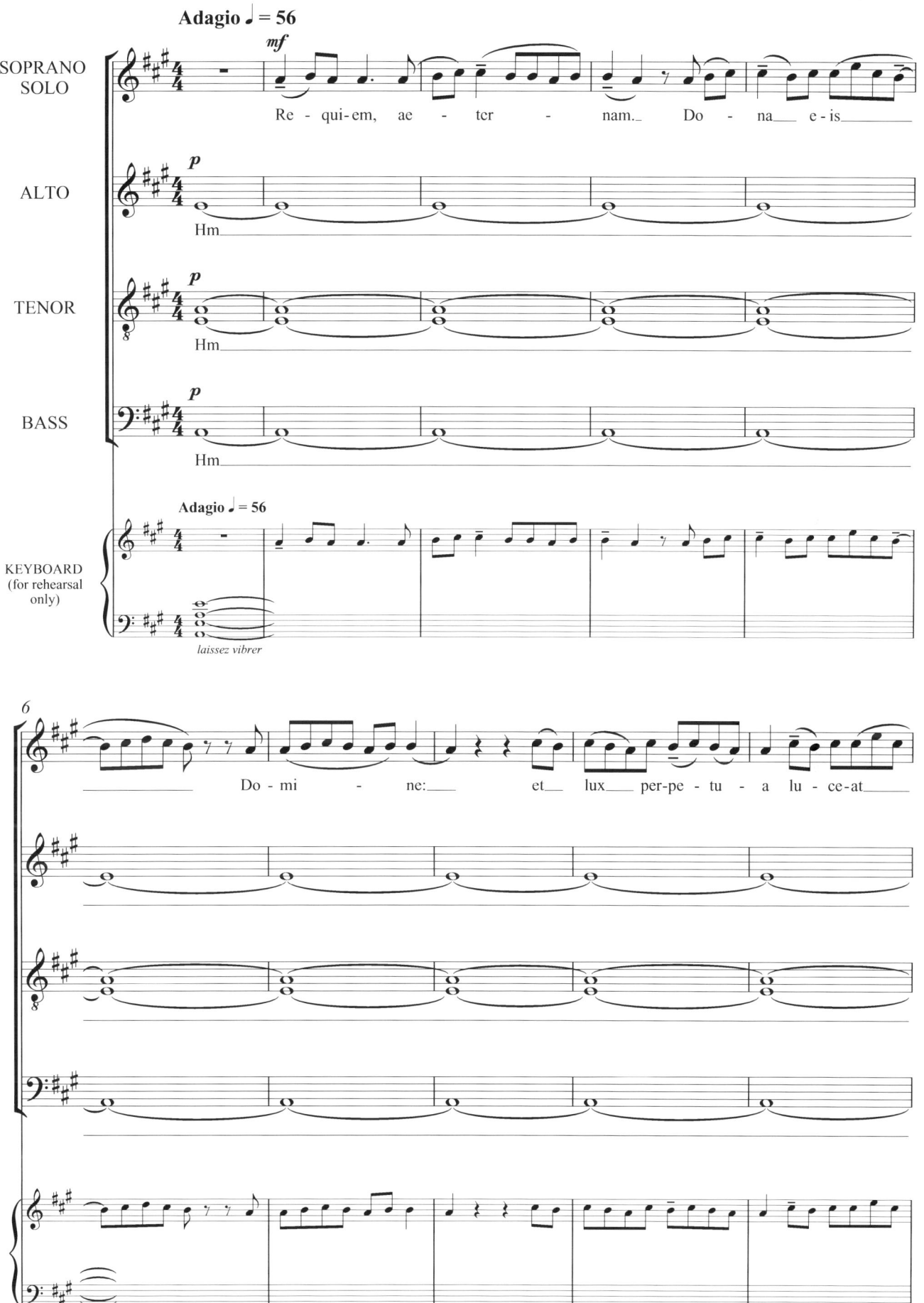

© 2017 by Peters Edition Ltd, London

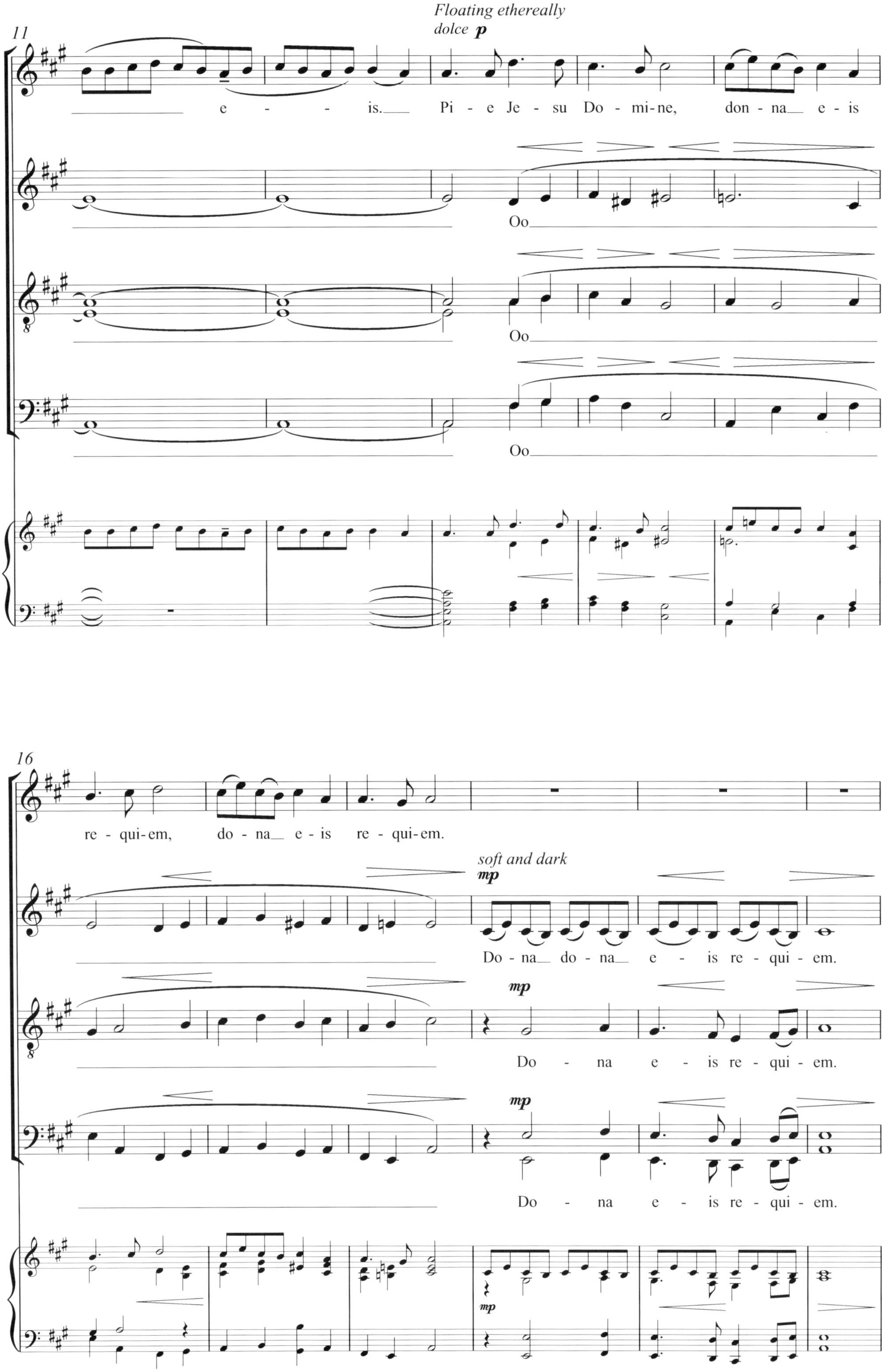
Floating ethereally
dolce p
11
e - - is. Pi - e Je - su Do - mi - ne, don - na e - is
Oo
Oo
Oo
16
re - qui - em, do - na e - is re - qui - em.
soft and dark
mp
Do - na do - na e - is re - qui - em.
mp
Do - na e - is re - qui - em.
mp
Do - na e - is re - qui - em.
mp

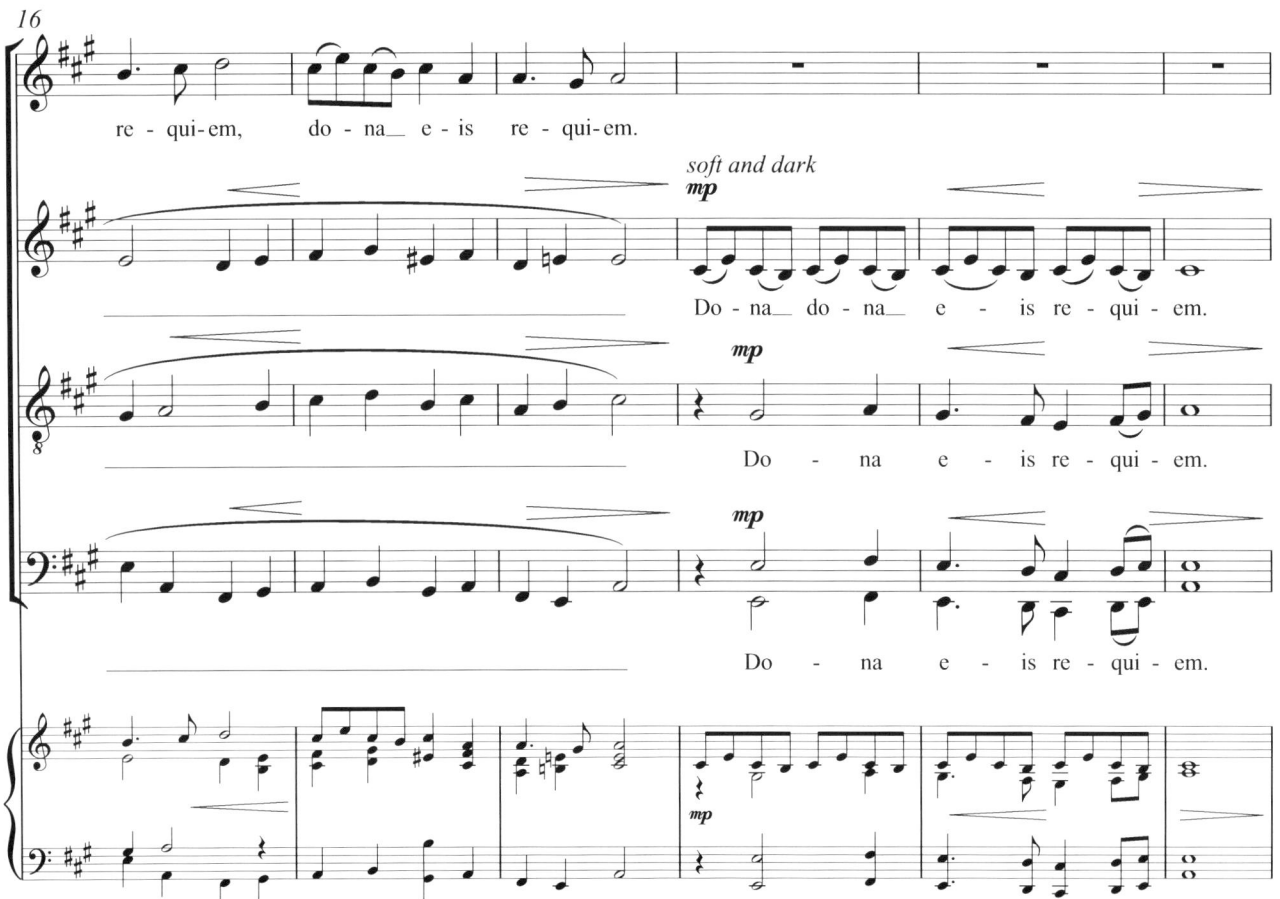

Pie Jesu | 41

42 | Pie Jesu

Edition Peters

44 | Pie Jesu

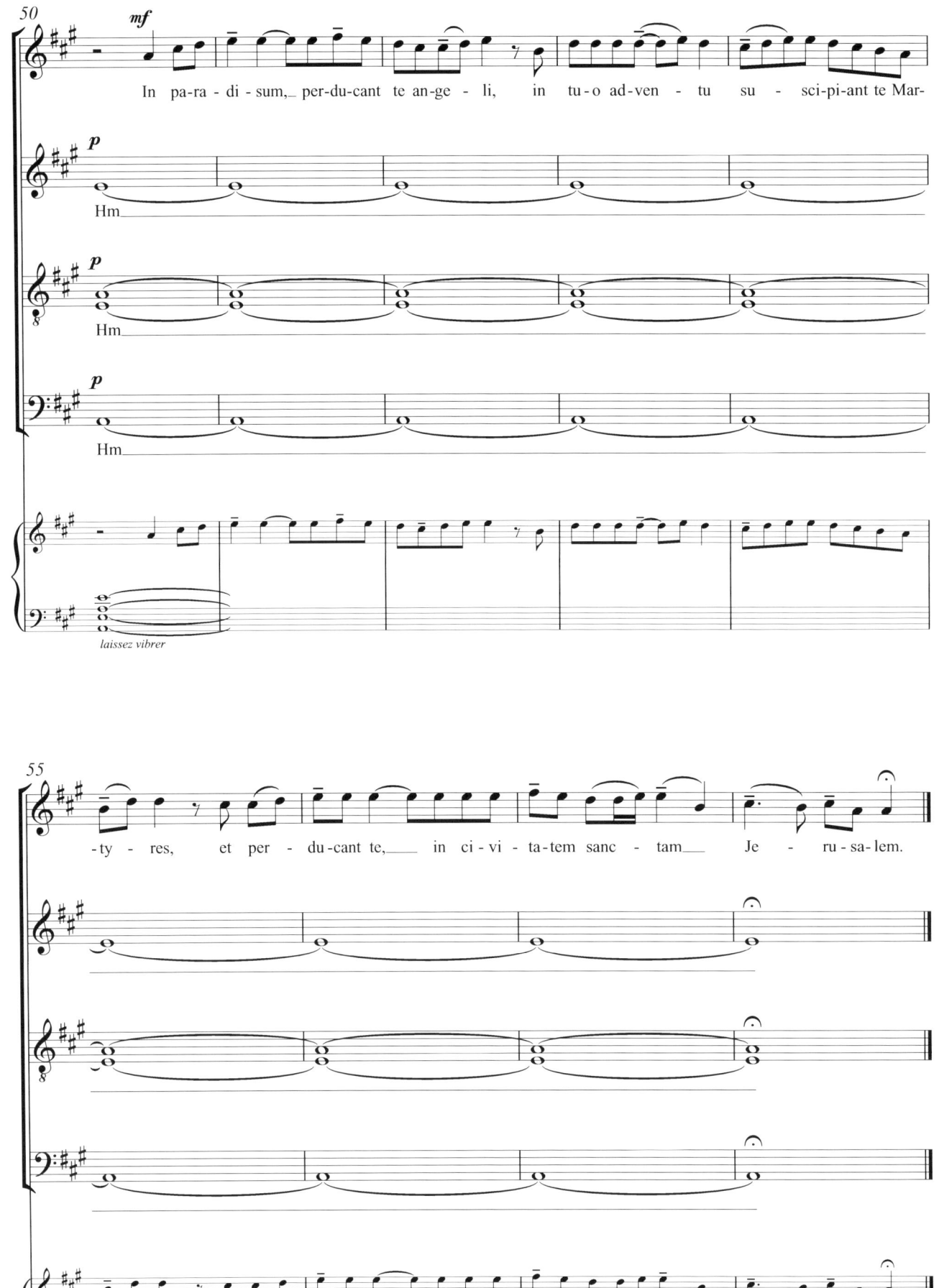

Price Tag

Words and Music by Claude Kelly, Bobby Ray Simmons Jr, Lukasz Gottwald and Jessica Cornish
arr. Andrea Halsey

© 2011 Studio Beast Music administered by Warner-Tamerlane Publishing Corp., Songs Of Universal, Inc., Ham Squad Music, Kasz Money Publishing, Prescription Songs, LLC and Sony/ATV Music Publishing (UK) Ltd
This arrangement Copyright © 2018 Studio Beast Music administered by Warner-Tamerlane Publishing Corp., Songs Of Universal, Inc., Ham Squad Music, Kasz Money Publishing, Prescription Songs, LLC and Sony/ATV Music Publishing (UK) Ltd
All rights on behalf of itself and Studio Beast Music administered by Warner-Tamerlane Publishing Corp, Warner/Chappell North America Ltd. Reprinted by permission of Faber Music Ltd and Alfred Music
All rights on behalf Ham Squad Music controlled and administered by Songs Of Universal, Inc., and Universal/MCA Music Ltd. Reprinted by permission of Music Sales Ltd, Hal Leonard Australia and Hal Leonard LLC
All rights on behalf of Kasz Money Publishing and Prescription Songs, LLC administered by Kobalt Music Publishing America, Inc. Reprinted by permission of Hal Leonard LLC
All rights on behalf of Sony/ATV Music Publishing UK Ltd administered by Sony/ATV Music Publishing LLC, 424 Church Street, Suite 1200, Nashville, TN 37219, USA.
Used by permission of JASRAC for Japan (Licence No. 1804545-801)
International Copyright Secured. All Rights Reserved.

7
night, When the sale comes first and the truth comes se - cond just stop for a min - ute and
dut du du dut du du dut du du dut du du
dut du du dut du du dut du du dut du du
dut du du dut du du dut du du dut du du
dut du du dut du du dut du du dut du du
9
smile,__ Why is ev -'ry - bo - dy so se - ri - ous? Act - ing so damn my -
dut du du dut du du dut du du dut du du
dut du du dut du du dut du du dut du du
dut du du dut du du dut du du dut du du
dut du du dut du du dut du du dut du du

Price Tag | 47

Edition Peters

Price Tag | 49

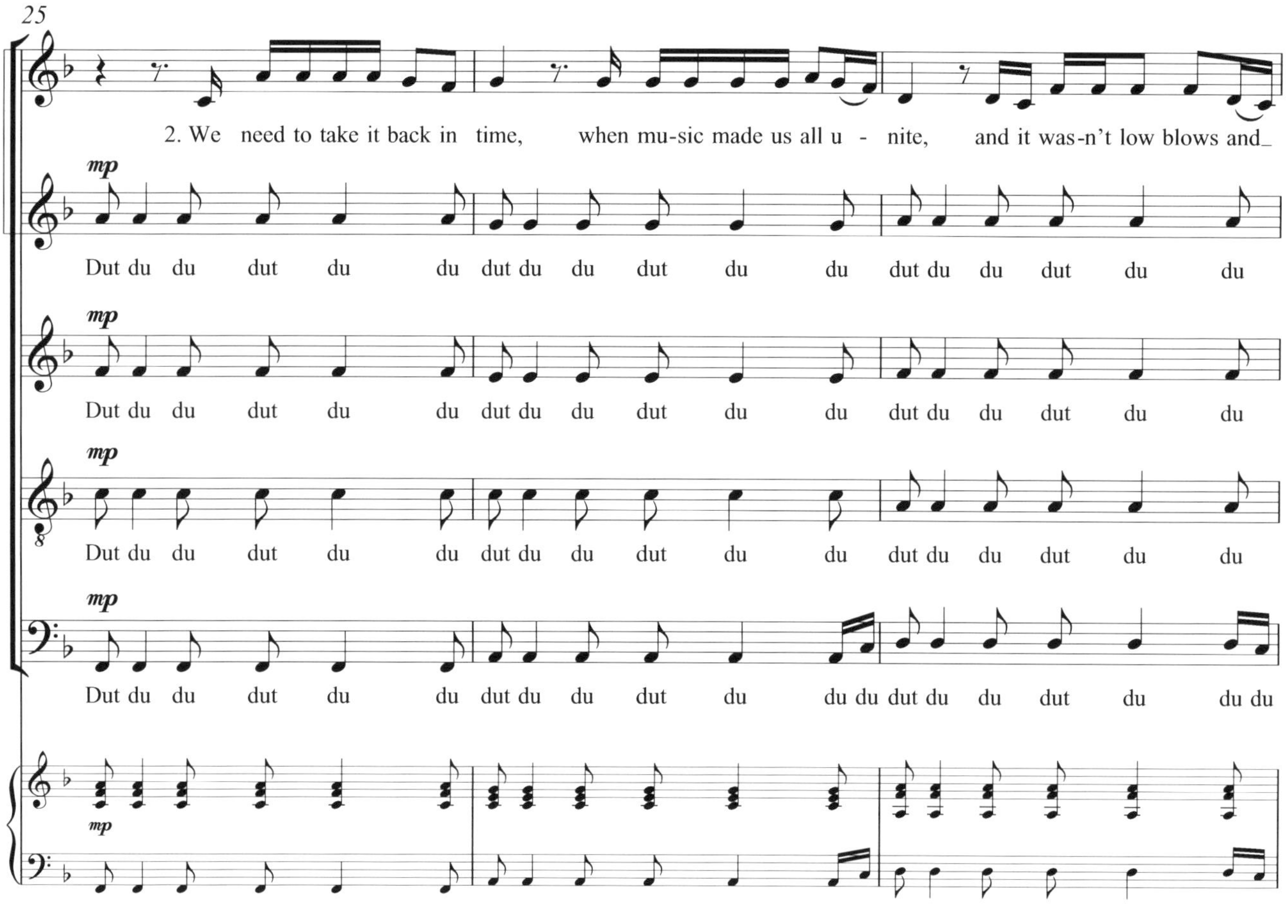
25
2. We need to take it back in time, when mu-sic made us all u - nite, and it was-n't low blows and_
mp
Dut du du dut du du dut du du dut du du dut du du dut du du
mp
Dut du du dut du du dut du du dut du du dut du du dut du du
mp
Dut du du dut du du dut du du dut du du dut du du dut du du
mp
Dut du du dut du du dut du du dut du du du dut du du dut du du du
mp

28
vi - de - o hoes, Am I the on - ly one get-ting tired?_ Why is ev -'ry - bo - dy so____
dut du du dut du du Dut du du dut du du
dut du du dut du du Dut du du dut du du
dut du du dut du du Dut du du dut du du
dut du du dut du du du du Dut du du dut du du

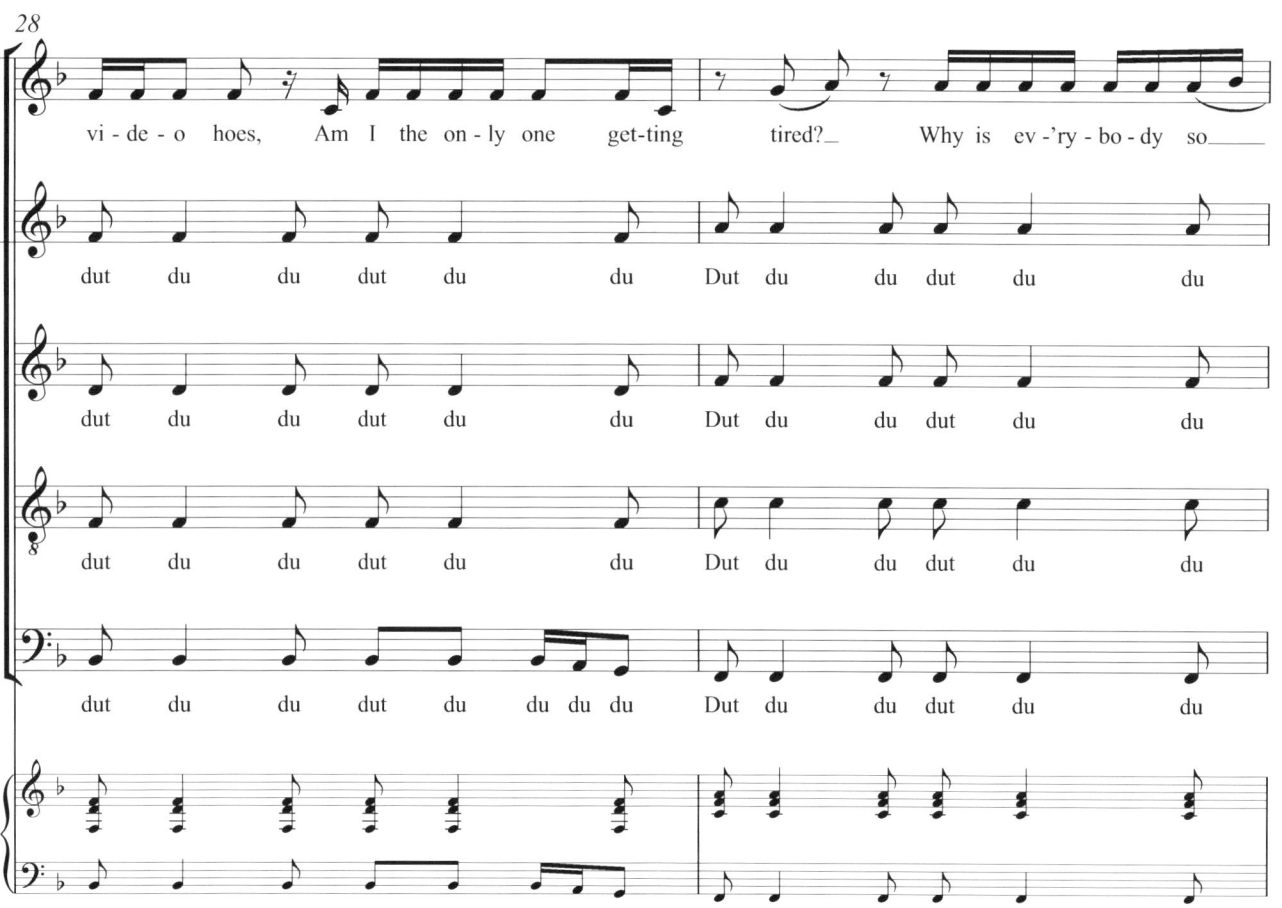

52 | Price Tag

Edition Peters

54 | Price Tag

42

b-bling, b-bling, wan-na make the world dance,_ for-get a-bout the price tag._

dat dah da dat dah da dat dah da dat dah da dat dah da dat dah da

dat dah da dat dah da dat dah da dat dah da dat dah da dat dah da

dat dah da dat dah da dat dah da dat dah da dat dah da dat dah da

dat dah da dat dah da dat dah da dat dah da dat dah da dat dah da

45 **Optional Solo Improvisation**

La la la la la_ la la la la dai_ da_ da_

Ba da ba da ba da ba da ba da ba da ba da ba da

Ba da ba da ba da ba da ba da ba da ba da ba da

Ba da ba da ba da ba da ba da ba da ba da ba da

Optional Bass Improvisation

Dm dm dm dm dm dm dm dm duh dm dm

Dm dm dm dm dm dm dm dm

Edition Peters

56 | Price Tag

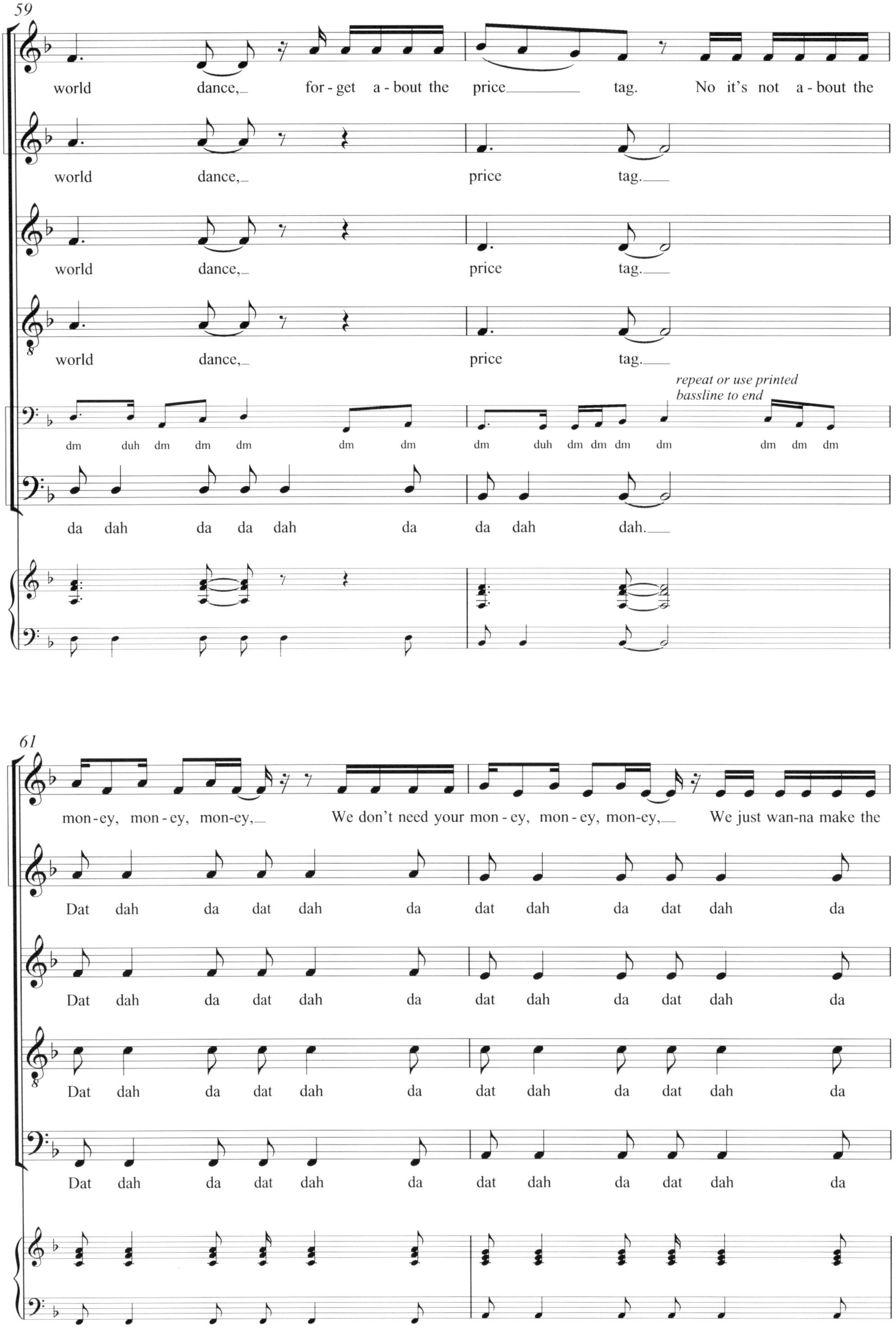
59
world dance, for-get a-bout the price tag. No it's not a-bout the
world dance, price tag.
world dance, price tag.
world dance, price tag.
repeat or use printed bassline to end
dm duh dm dm dm dm dm dm duh dm dm dm dm dm dm dm
da dah da da dah da da dah dah.
61
mon-ey, mon-ey, mon-ey, We don't need your mon-ey, mon-ey, mon-ey, We just wan-na make the
Dat dah da dat dah da dat dah da dat dah da
Dat dah da dat dah da dat dah da dat dah da
Dat dah da dat dah da dat dah da dat dah da
Dat dah da dat dah da dat dah da dat dah da

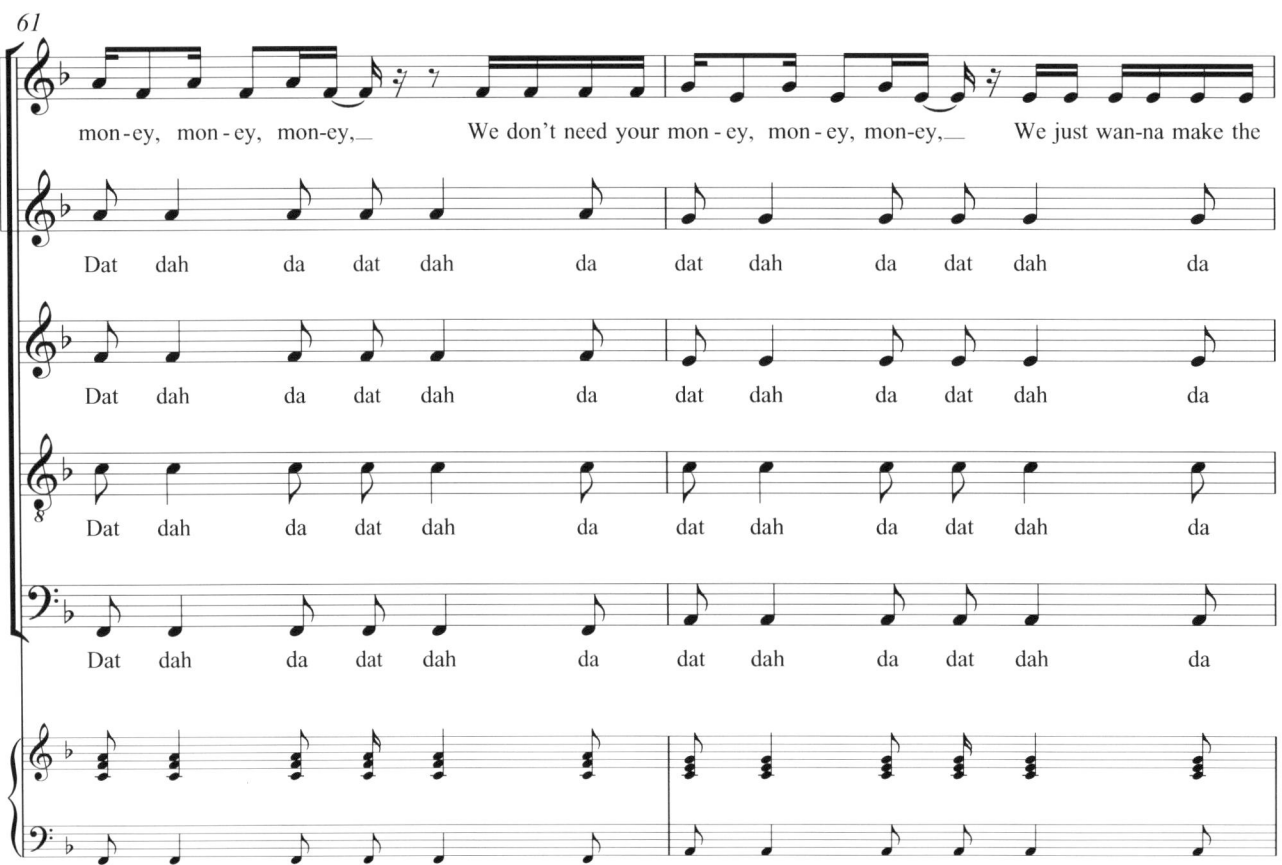

Strong

Words and Music by Hannah Reid, Dominic Major and Daniel Rothman
arr. Emily Dickens and Dingle Yandell

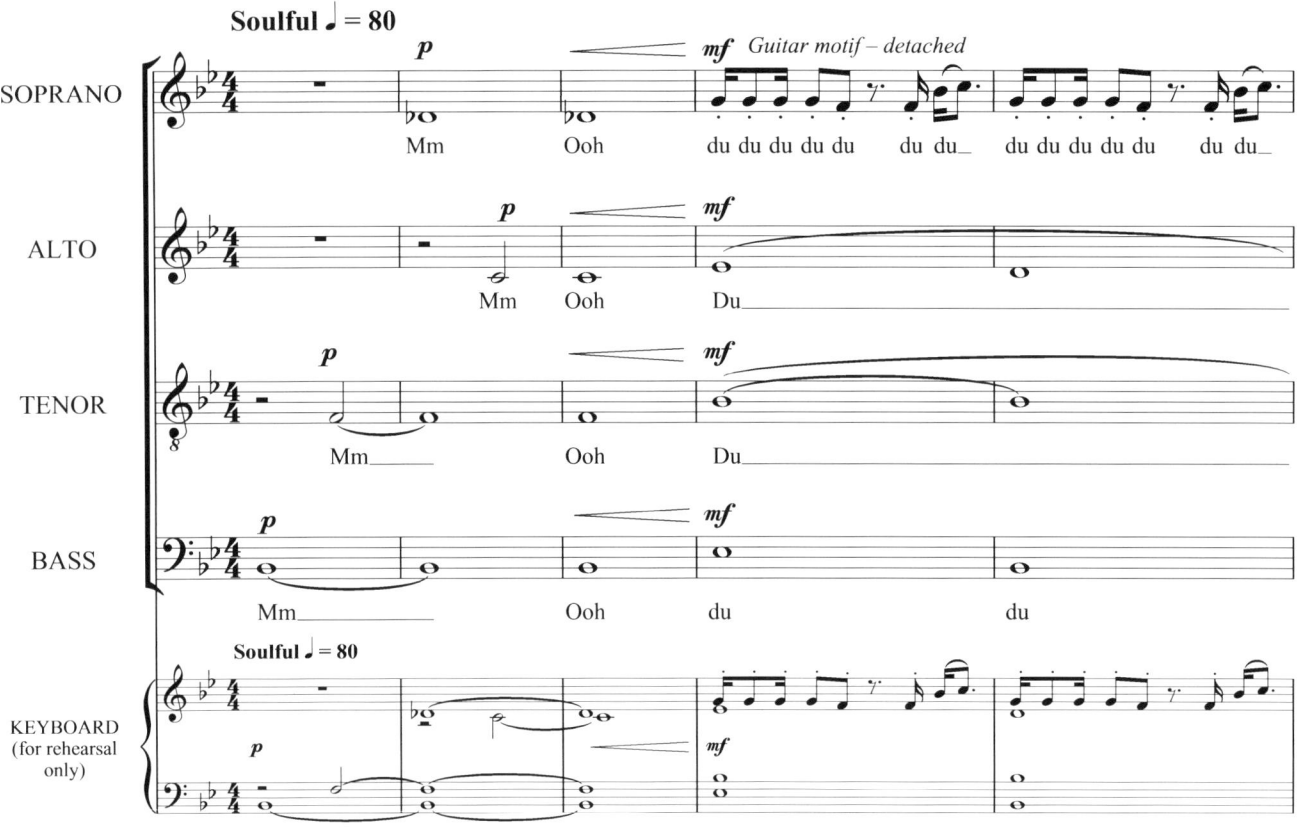

© 2013 Warner/Chappell Music Ltd, London W8 5DA
All Rights in the U.S. and Canada administered by WB Music Corp.
Reproduced by permission of Faber Music Ltd and Alfred Music
All Rights Reserved.

64 | Strong

Edition Peters

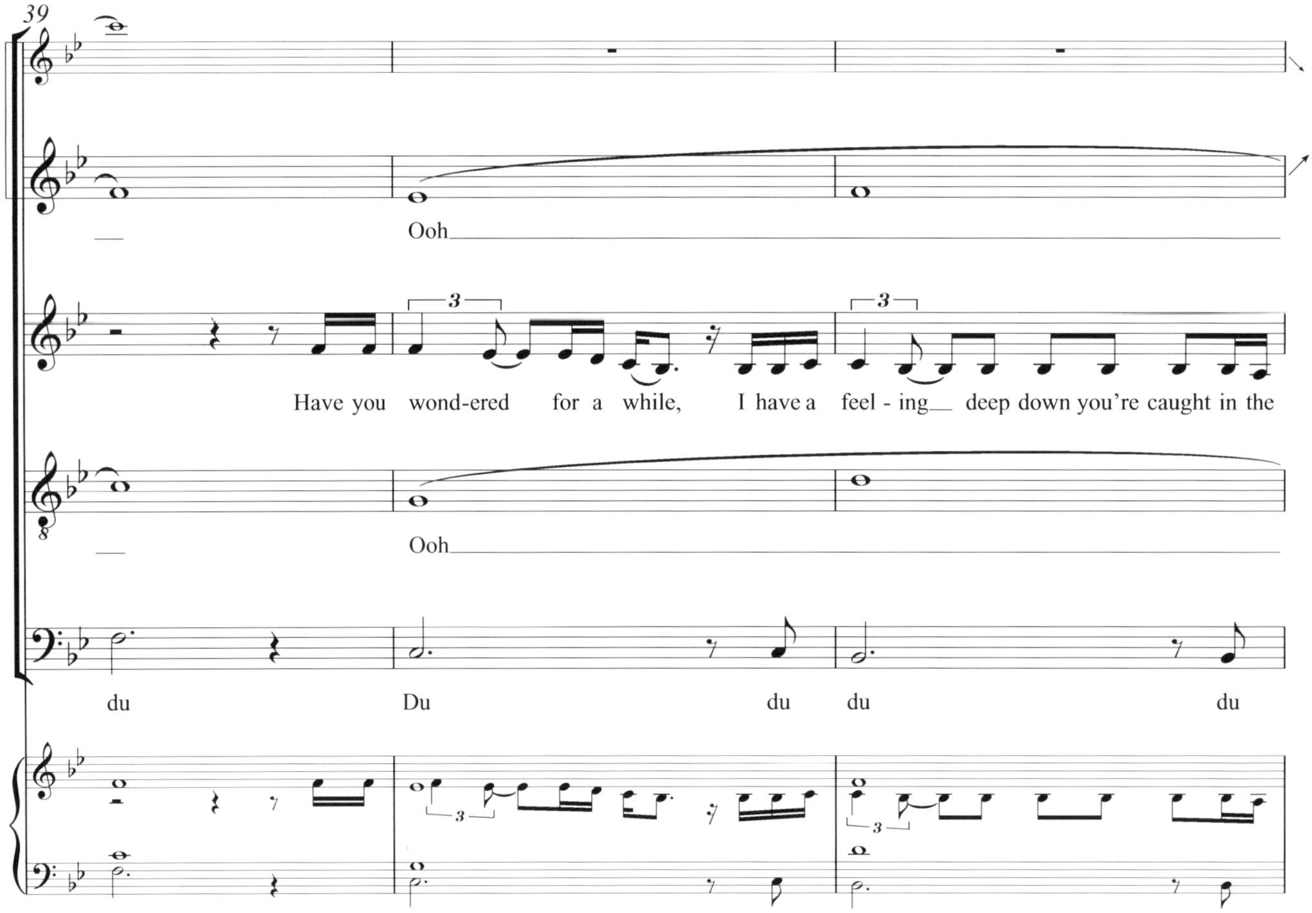
39
Ooh
Have you wond-ered for a while, I have a feel - ing deep down you're caught in the
Ooh
du Du du du du

42
mf
And a li - on, a li - on roars, would
mid- dle, mid- dle, mid- dle.
La
La
du du du Du du du du

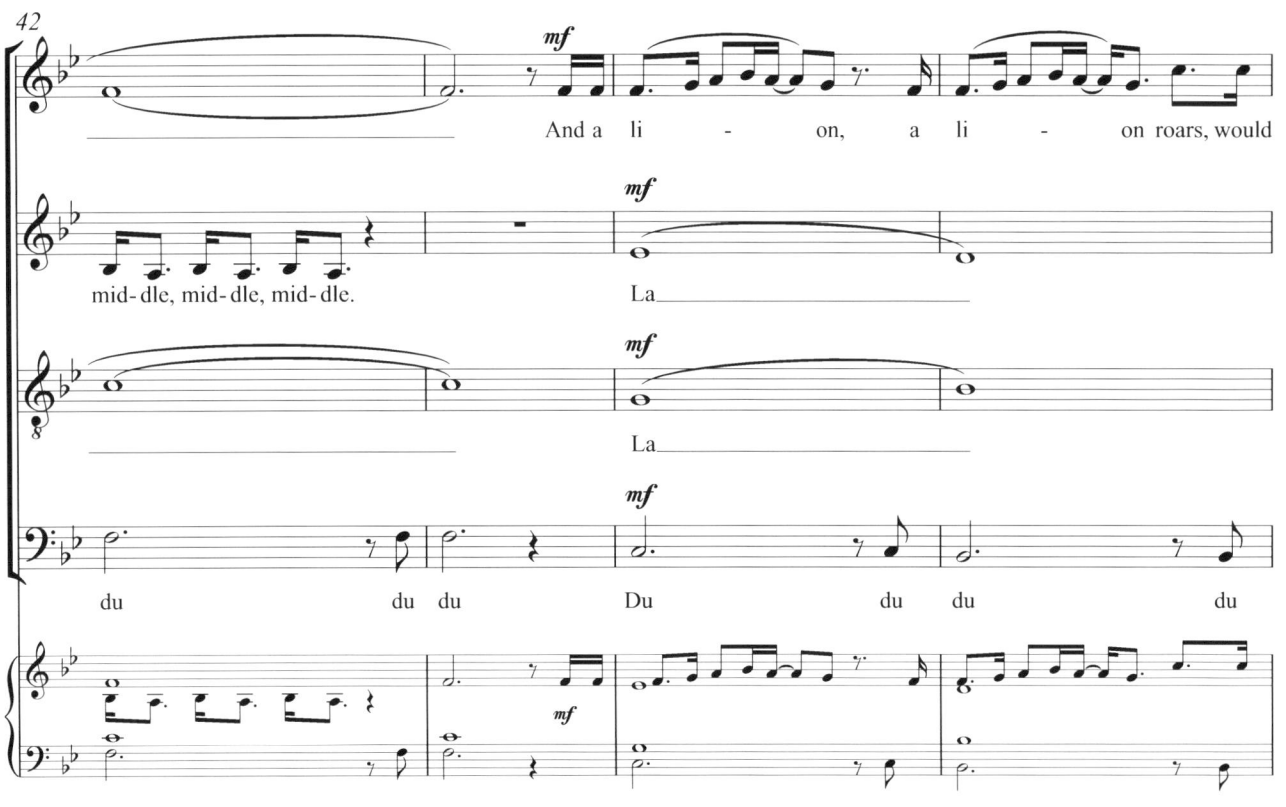

46
cresc.
you not list-en?_ If a child,_ a child_ cries would
Ooh_ La_
Ooh_ La_
du du du du du Du du du du
cresc.
50
mp
Yeah, I might seem so strong, yeah I might speak so long,_ I've nev-er
f
you not for-give them? Yeah, I might seem so strong, yeah I might speak so long, I've nev-er
Ooh_ Ah_
Ooh_ du du du_ du du du du du du du_ du du du du
du du du du du du_ du_ du du_ du_
Dm K dm dm K Dm K dm dm K

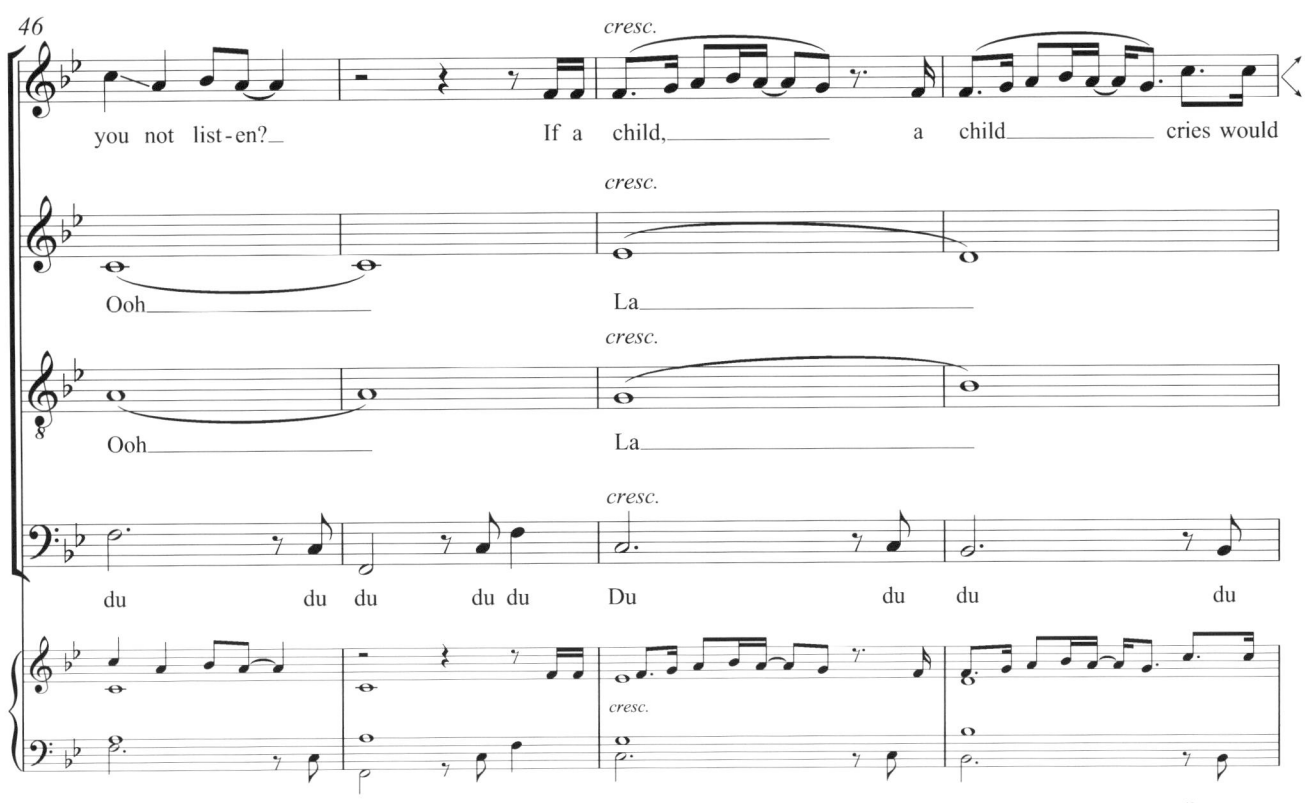

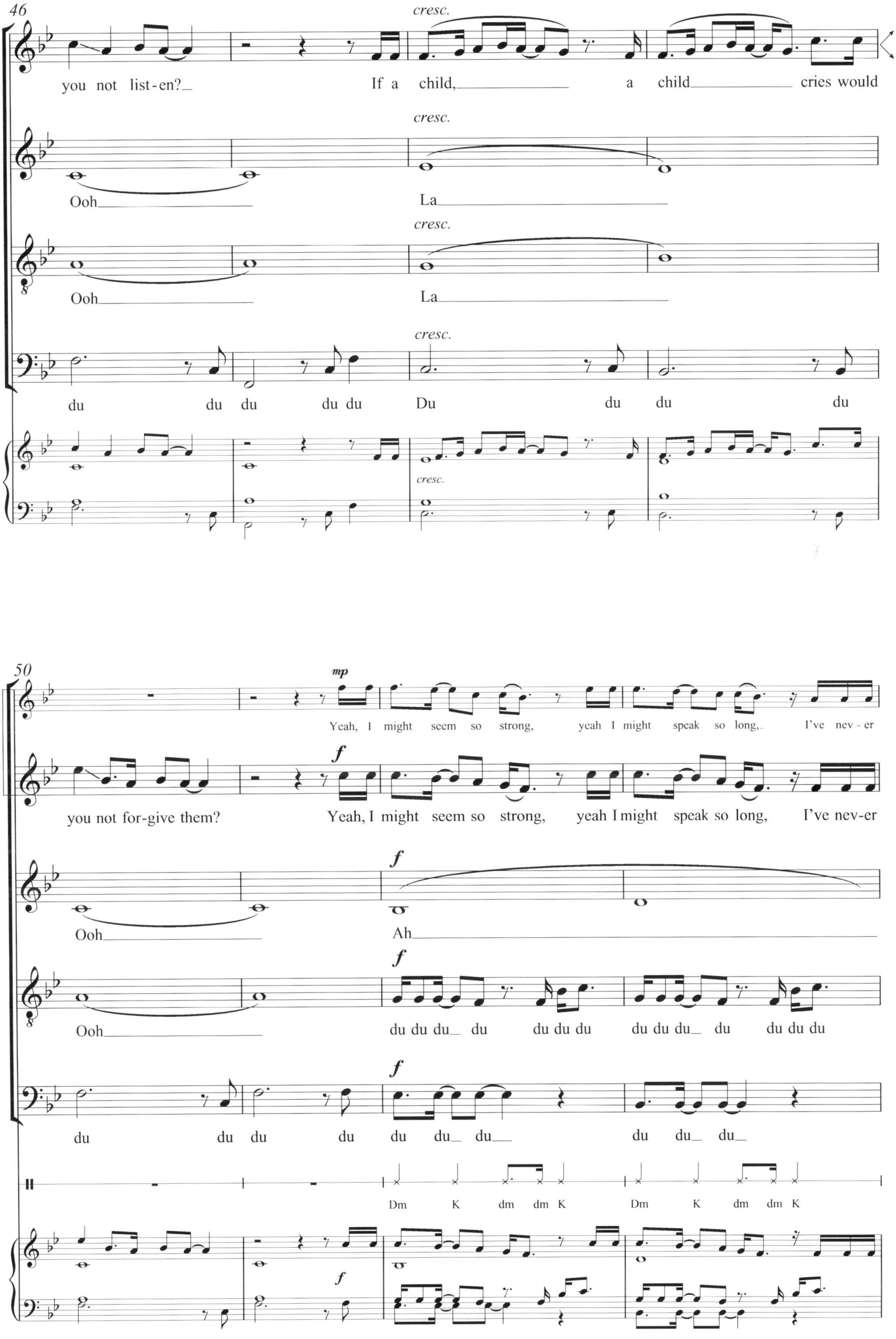

68 | Strong

Underneath the Stars

Underneath the Stars | 73

74 | Underneath the Stars

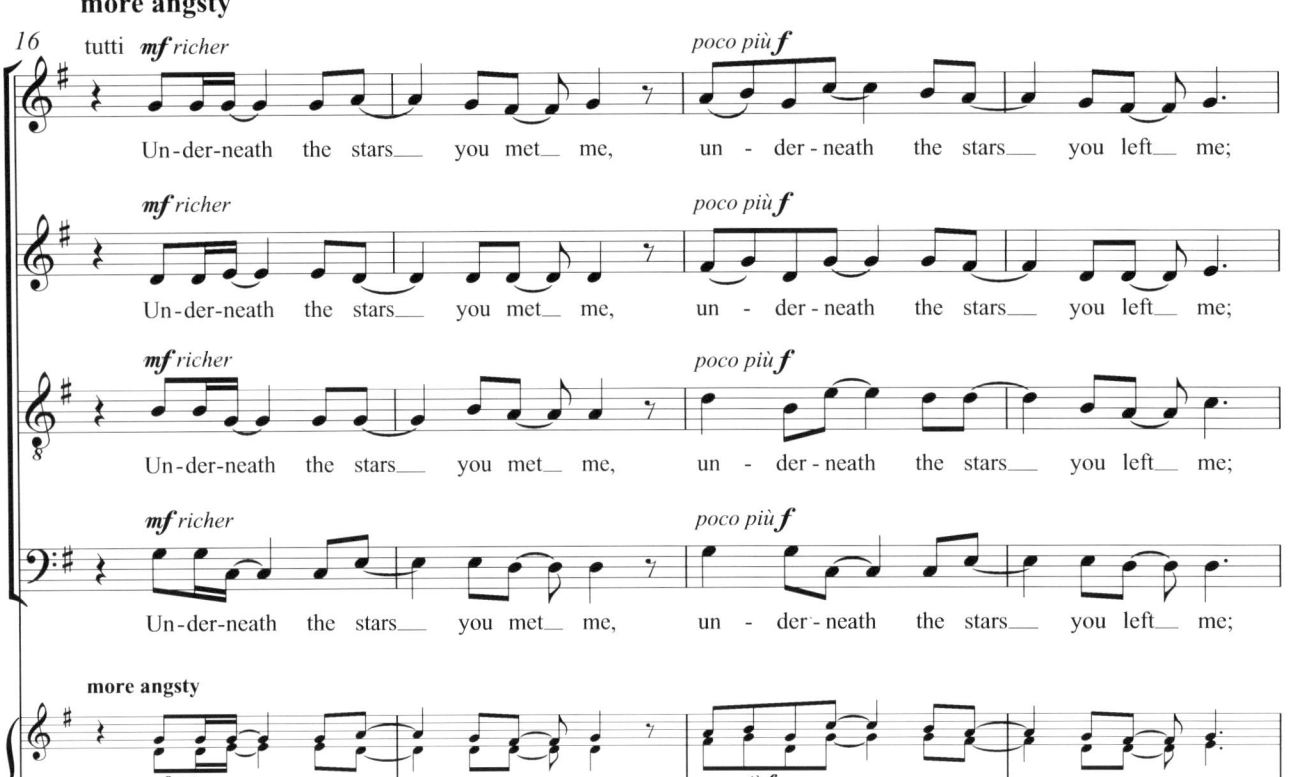

Edition Peters

Underneath the Stars | 75

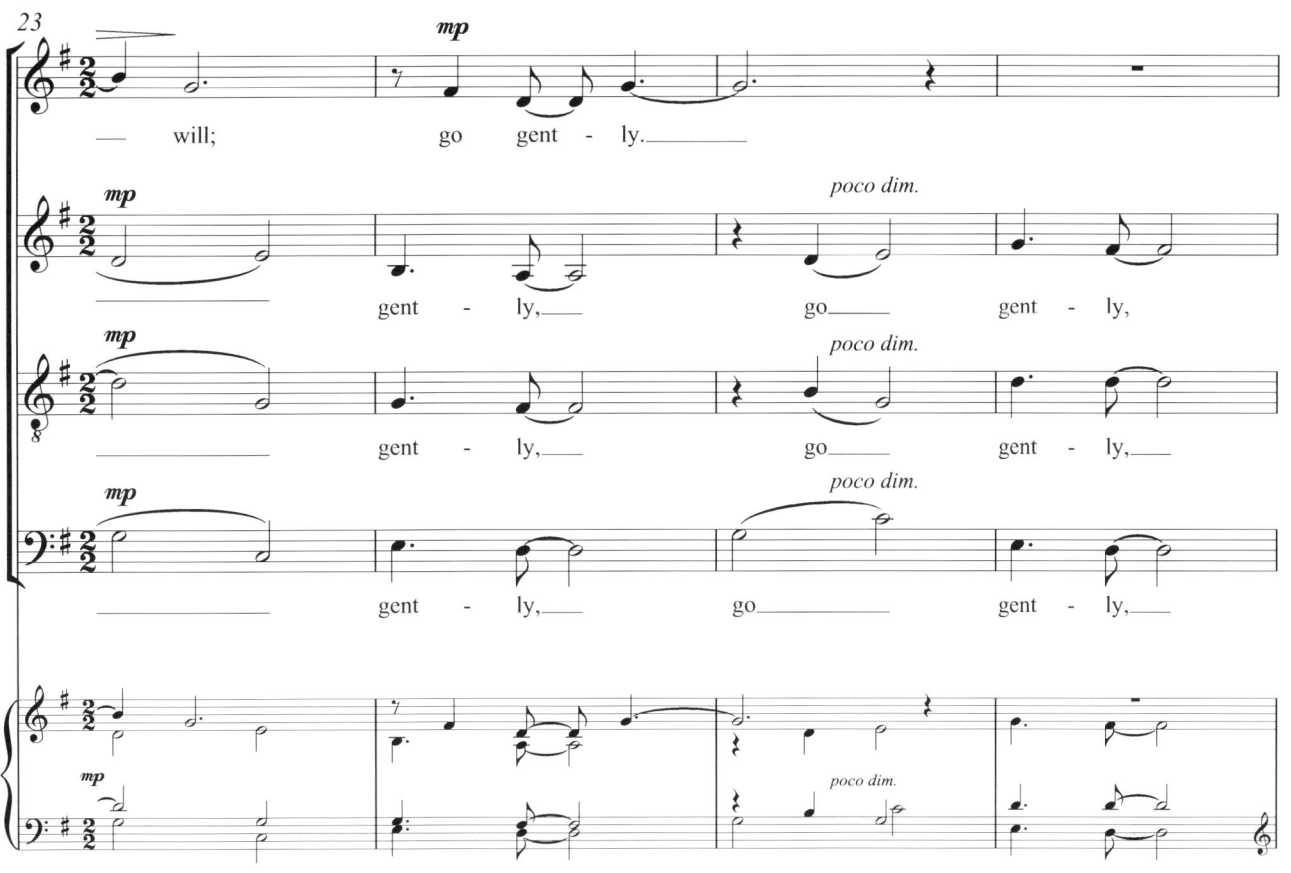

Edition Peters

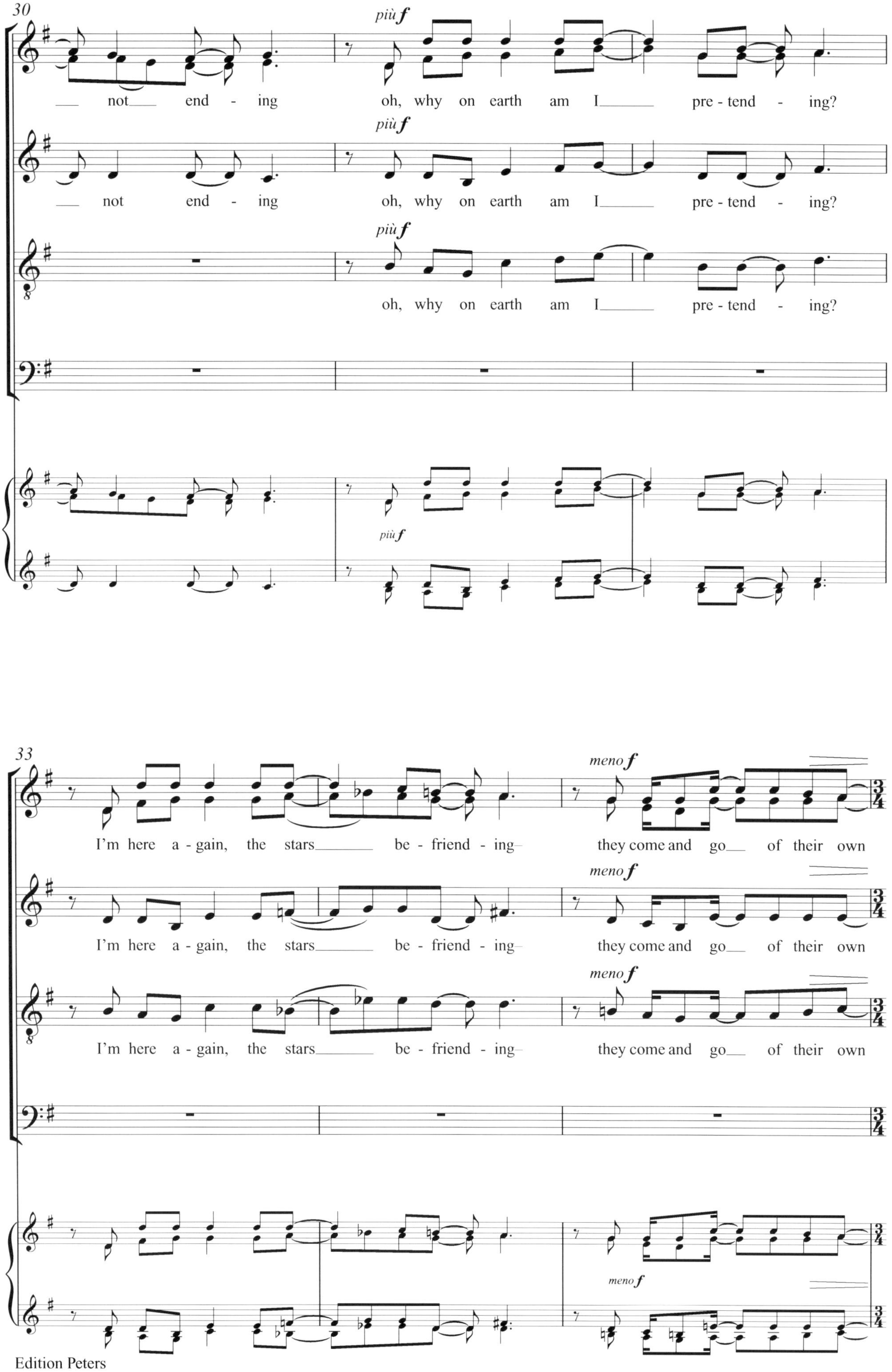

76 | Underneath the Stars

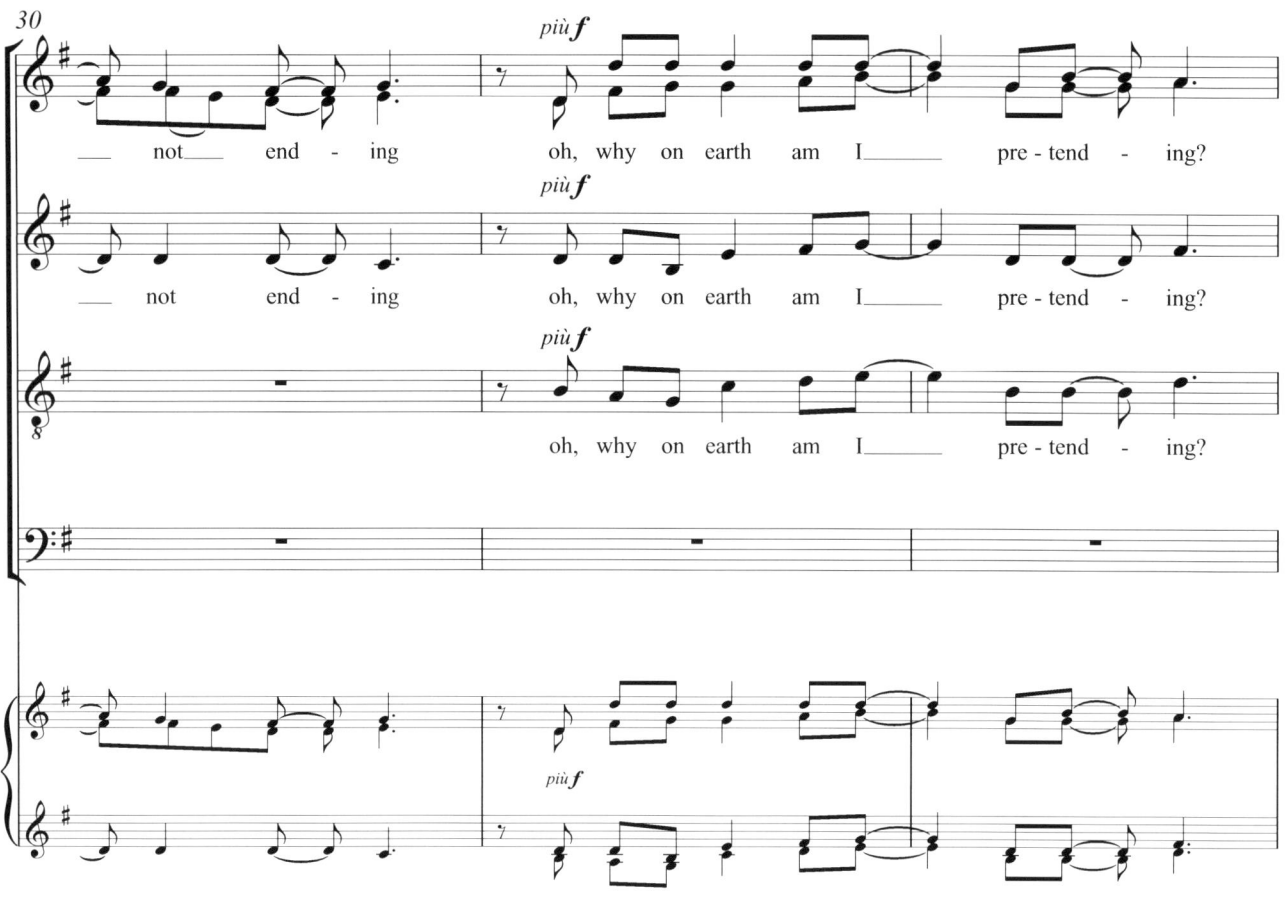

Underneath the Stars | 77

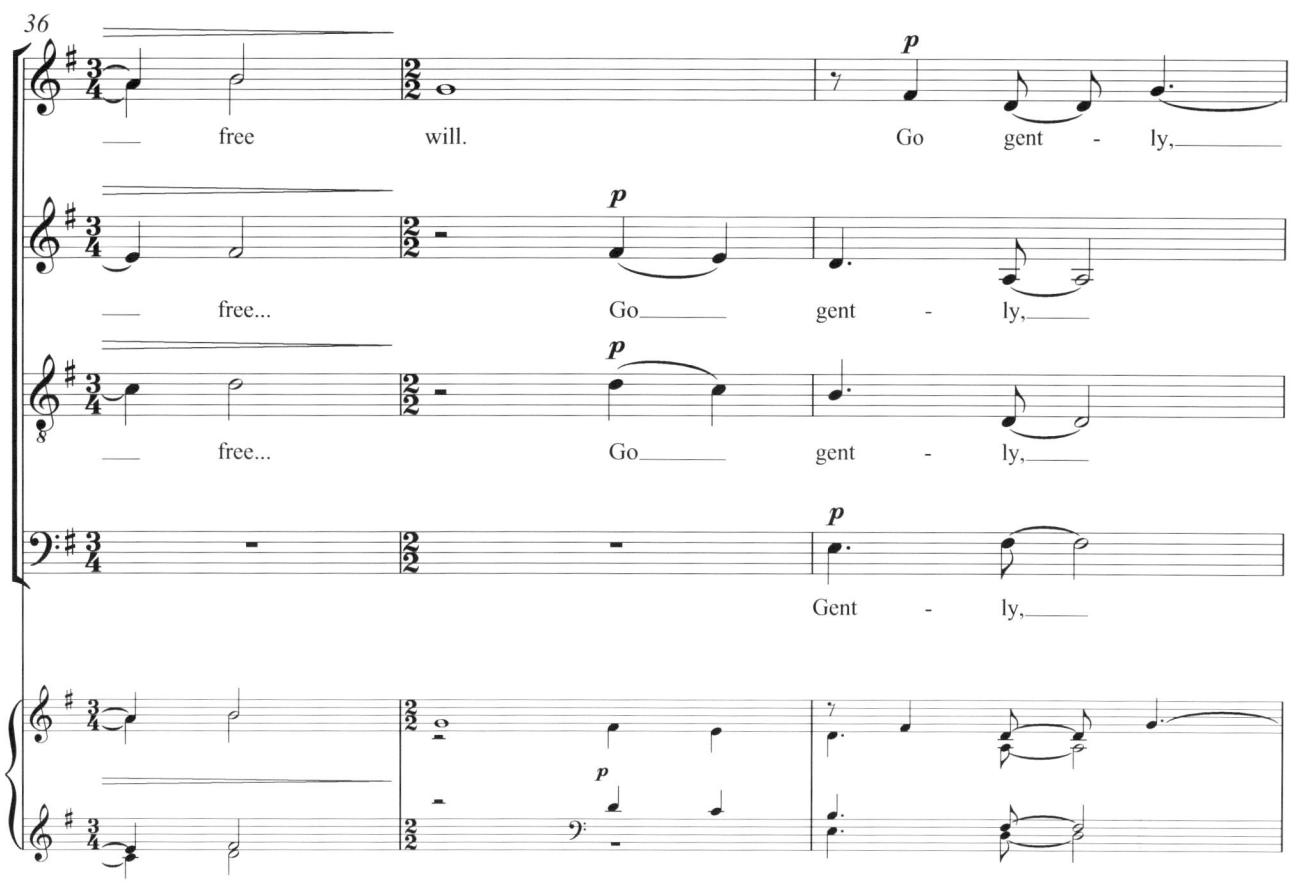

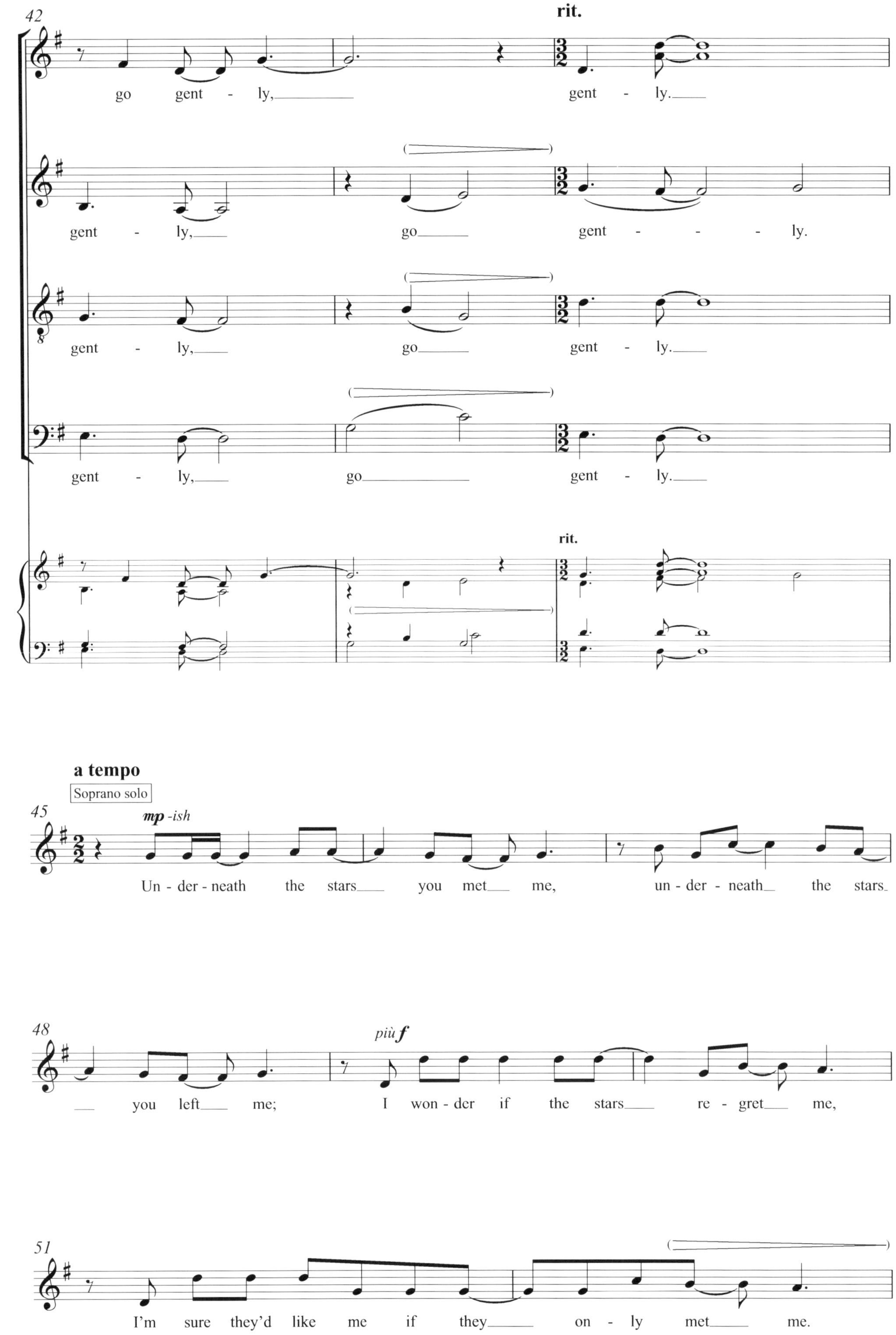

78 | Underneath the Stars

Edition Peters

Underneath the Stars | 79

Edition Peters